The
GOOD
BEE

A Celebration of Bees
and How to Save Them

Alison Benjamin
& Brian McCallum

Michael O'Mara Books Limited

First published in Great Britain in 2019 by
Michael O'Mara Books Limited
9 Lion Yard
Tremadoc Road
London SW4 7NQ

Copyright © Alison Benjamin and Brian McCallum 2019

All rights reserved. You may not copy, store, distribute, transmit, reproduce
or otherwise make available this publication (or any part of it) in any form,
or by any means (electronic, digital, optical, mechanical, photocopying,
recording or otherwise), without the prior written permission of the
publisher. Any person who does any unauthorized act in relation to this
publication may be liable to criminal prosecution and civil claims for
damages.

A CIP catalogue record for this book is available from the British Library.

Papers used by Michael O'Mara Books Limited are natural, recyclable
products made from wood grown in sustainable forests. The manufacturing
processes conform to the environmental regulations of the country of
origin.

ISBN: 978-1-78929-083-7 in hardback print format

ISBN: 978-1-78929-084-4 in ebook format

4 5 6 7 8 9 10

Cover design by Claire Cater

Typeset by K DESIGN, Winscombe, Somerset

Illustrations by James Nunn

Printed and bound by CPI Group (UK) Ltd, Croydon, CR0 4YY

www.mombooks.com

MIX
Paper from
responsible sources
FSC
www.fsc.org   FSC® C020471

Contents

Introduction

In 2006, we embarked on a journey to become urban beekeepers. We'd heard that bees were in peril in the countryside, where their habitats were being destroyed, and that towns and cities could provide a refuge. We wanted to give bees a home in the overgrown garden of the west London flat we lived in at the time.

All we knew about bees back then was that they needed saving and made honey. We had a lot to learn. We went on a beginners' course with the London Beekeepers' Association and found to our astonishment that bees come in many shapes and sizes: they are not all round, plump and stripy like the bumblebees we'd seen in our garden. The type of bees that are kept in hives are slender and waspish-looking. Even more surprisingly, we learned that these hive-dwelling bees are one of the few that make honey. Intrigued, we put our names down to receive a starter colony of honeybees in early summer. We bought a hive and all the equipment, including two bee suits, and eagerly waited. Finally, we got the call to come and collect our bees.

That day in June ignited a passion. We became absorbed in the bees' comings and goings, their fascinating social structures – the queen bee, her female workers and male drones living together in the hive, their labours strictly demarcated to maximize the efficiency of the colony – and their communication through smell and dance.

The honeybees became a catalyst, opening our eyes to the workings of nature; how the tiniest fluctuation in the temperature, humidity or availability of flowers could trigger changes in the behaviour of insects with whom they have co-evolved for 100 million years. Moreover, honeybees introduced us to the astonishing variety of bees on the planet. We now know that there are some 25,000 recorded bee species worldwide, most of which live alone and don't make honey. We have begun to acquaint ourselves with some of these amazing, often unnoticed bees nesting in nooks and crannies. They don't conform to the image most of us have of a good bee. But once we got to know these less familiar creatures, with their distinctive markings and behavioural idiosyncrasies, they became every bit as alluring and beelike.

Many of the bees you will meet in this book have a solitary disposition, nesting alone, although often next door to each other. These wild, solitary bees are essential

pollinators. Together with the few social species, they pollinate one in every three mouthfuls we eat, as well as feeding birds and animals in the complex food chain that sustains nature's delicately balanced ecosystems and is part of earth's wondrous biodiversity.

This book also delves into bees' special relationship with Homo sapiens. Since humankind began honey hunting 20,000 years ago, bees have provided food, sweetness, candlelight and medicine. Now they are giving us a sign, like the canary in the coalmine, that their future is threatened and, with it, life on Earth as we know it.

We will explore the reasons for the bees' decline, from habitat loss to pesticides and climate change, including the culprits behind honeybees' widely reported colony collapse disorder. But we will also be striking a more hopeful note, looking at various steps that farmers, businesses – and you – can take to help reverse their fortunes. Some progress is already being made: a few pesticides are already banned in some parts of the world, and there are projects to restore bee-friendly habitats and even reintroduce wild bees.

But you can't save what you don't love, and you can't love what you don't know. So, we hope this book will first and foremost help people fall in love with the bees around them. Perhaps, if we can put names and faces to the long-ignored but uniquely alluring solitary bees, with their hairy feet, ginger tufts and ingenious home-building techniques, then we'll stand a better chance of saving nature's master pollinator – and, in the process, ourselves.

CHAPTER 1
Bees and Nature

✦ Where do bees come from? ✦

When we see a bee visiting a flower, we are observing an act of nature that has been playing out across the planet for more than 100 million years. Back then, the continents were still forming; India had yet to collide with Asia and create the Himalayas; the K-T extinction event and the loss of the dinosaurs was still to happen; birds and mammals were just beginning to emerge; and humans weren't even a speck on the horizon.

It is not possible to perfectly describe events that unfolded over thousands of millennia, but fossil records provide a picture of the past that can be pieced together and which gives us clues about when, why and how bees came into existence.

The story begins with the first flowering plants.

Sexual reproduction is not simple if you're rooted to

the spot and your mate is some distance away. Plants, unlike animals, don't have the ability to wander around looking for suitable mates, so they require the help of a go-between to bring the two sexes together.

It seems that around 150 million years ago, the planet's plant life hooked up with the help of the wind. In this method of pollination, the wind carries a grain of pollen

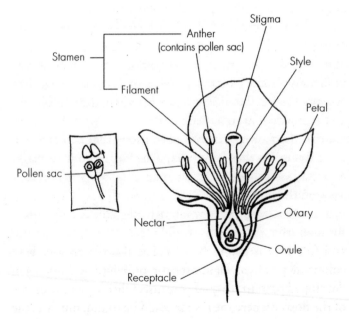

Flower parts

from the male part of one flower (the stamen) some distance to connect with the female part of another (the stigma). This is a somewhat unreliable method to spread your genes and requires the production of a huge amount of pollen, most of which will miss its target. Today, only around 20 per cent of plant species, such as cereals and grasses, still rely on the wind for pollination.

But nature soon devised a more efficient way for plants to have sex: one that involves an animal or insect to transport pollen. By this method – biotic pollination – the insect that touches the flower head picks up the pollen and moves it to another flower head, where the pollen touches the stigma and fertilizes the plant. This method of animal-assisted pollination is much more effective and its development was responsible for the proliferation of wonderfully colourful and aromatic flowering plants.

The insects' services proved so useful that plants began to compete for their attention. They began to offer them a sweet, sugary gift called nectar as a reward for their assistance. To advertise their wares, the flowers began producing a huge variety of rich perfumes that wafted through the air. Insects caught the tantalizing aroma and followed it to the flowers. The flowers also evolved colourful petals as signposts for pollinators; some even developed patterns to guide the insect directly to the centre of the flower where the nectar could be found, much as the segments of a dartboard point to the bullseye.

✦ What is a bee? ✦

Many insects, including butterflies, moths, and beetles, small birds such as hummingbirds, and some mammals, including fruit bats, drink nectar to fuel their flight and brush up against pollen while they are enjoying their energy drink. But bees generally do a much better job of pollination. Why? Because they have evolved to become totally dependent on flowering plants for their food.

Bees are members of the order of insects known as *Hymenoptera*. The name is derived from the Greek words *hymen*, meaning membrane, and *ptera*, meaning wings. This order includes ants, and wasps from which bees evolved. While wasps obtain protein for their young by feeding them fresh meat and carrion, bees became vegetarian and developed a taste for pollen – an essential part of a flowering plant's reproductive system. Just as a caterpillar transforms into a butterfly after spinning a silk cocoon, bee eggs hatch into larvae, which then turn into pupae and metamorphose into adult bees. But the larvae aren't able to develop into healthy adult bees without eating protein-rich pollen, so bees have developed ways of collecting pollen for themselves, as well as spreading it for the plants with amazing precision.

The poet Kahlil Gibran (1883–1931) beautifully described the symbiotic relationship between bee and flower that ensures both survive: 'To the bee, a flower is the fountain of life, and to the flower the bee is a messenger of love.' Bees are the flowering plants' very own Eros. Is it any wonder that the love god is portrayed with wings?

An astonishing 25,000 or so species of bee have evolved to pollinate flowering plants. To put that in perspective, there are around 10,000 species of birds, and around 5,400 different mammals. Many of these bee species don't conform to the popular image of a bee. Some are large and plump, others are skinny and small. There are striped ones and shiny, metallic, colourful ones. Many of us mistakenly believe that all bees make honey and sting. But only one genus, or group, of bees does both: *Apis*, the honeybee. Many bees can sting, but a few bite, or spray their predators with acid instead. There are short-lived bees and bees that live for years. A few bees live together in colonies of up to 100,000, but the majority nest alone. There are bees that lick human sweat; short-tongued and long-tongued bees; bees that nest in the ground, in trees, or hollow plant stems; and bees that have given up on making their own nest but instead take over other bees' homes. But wherever there are flowering plants, from windswept mountaintops to humid jungles and arid deserts, as well as our gardens and backyards, there will be bees to pollinate them. We have bees to thank for the aesthetic beauty and heavenly scent of the flowering world.

✦ The bee's toolkit ✦

Although many of the 25,000 species don't make honey and rarely sting, they all share some common traits that makes the bee nature's master pollinator.

Like all insects, bees have a head, thorax and abdomen. But what sets the bee apart is its hairy body, covered in feathery, branched filaments. Bees evolved their furry coats to pick up powdery pollen from the flower's anther (the tip of the stamen, the male part of the flower). Not only are the hairs ideally shaped for this task but they are also electrically charged. The positive charge of the bees' hair attracts the slightly negatively charged pollen so that it jumps off the anther on to the bee when it is busy rummaging around the flower head in search of its food. The rest of a bee's body has also structurally adapted to the job of pollination, providing it with an extensive toolkit for crafting an existence from the floral world, better than any other animal.

On its head, a bee has five eyes, again like most insects: three simple eyes on the top of the head that detect changes in light and tell it which way is up, so that it doesn't fly upside down; and two large compound eyes on the side that give it overlapping fields of vision with which to judge depth and distance. The large eyes have around 5,000 tiny lenses that allow bees to detect nectar

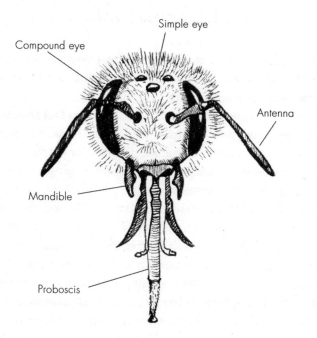

Bee's head

guides on petals from afar and to see polarized light, so that they can navigate by the sun, even on cloudy days. Bees don't register slow movements and they perceive a slightly different spectrum of colour than humans do: shifted towards ultraviolet and more sensitive to yellows and blues. This means that flowers that might seem plain to us can appear as a dazzling array of yellows and purples with ultraviolet nectar guides to a bee. They can even detect a flower's slight change in colour when it is out of nectar, a signal to the bee to visit another flower for its food.

Bee antennae have evolved to pick up flower scent a hundred times better than we do. Their acute olfactory senses can detect a complex range of perfumes far downwind of the plant, and they will fly along the scented airways to find their treasures.

Given their acute sense of smell, it's not surprising that pheromones play an important role in the life of bees. They can use these special chemical signs, secreted from their glands, to locate their nests, recognize their kin, and attract mates. Foreign pheromones alert them to intruders. Recent research shows that some bees even have pheromones that make their feet smell, to remind them which flowers they have visited. It is thought that the pheromone might inform other visiting bees to bypass the flower, for while the smell of the first visiting bee is lingering there, it means that its nectaries (the glands where it stores nectar) are empty. By the time the pheromone has dissipated, the flower will have had time to refill for the next visitor.

Because the nectaries are often tucked away in the centre of the plant, bees have developed a special straw-

Nectar guides

like mouthpart called a proboscis that allows them to probe deep inside the flower and suck up the liquid. The length of the proboscis depends on the flowers they have evolved to feed from and pollinate. Some flowers have deep bell-like or tubular petals for which a long tongue is required, while others have flat, open petals that act as a landing board for bees and offer a more easily accessible drink.

Instead of teeth, bees have two powerful mandibles which work like pincers to hold, bite and manipulate various materials to construct their nests.

The bee's thorax is the engine that powers its flight muscles. Bees have two pairs of wings that can interlock and fold together to allow them to squeeze into small spaces. In flight, they beat at an astonishing 200 beats or more per second. Some bees have evolved particularly strong muscles to carry heavy loads of nectar and pollen – more than half their own body weight – over long distances.

The bee's six legs have hooks for hanging onto the edges of petals, and pads that allow it to walk upside down. The front legs can be used to clean its sensitive antennae. In some species of bee, the back legs feature special baskets for transporting pollen. The middle legs can help brush the pollen into each basket, or corbicula. Other species of bee have dense hairs on the underside of their abdomen, in a tuft called a scopa, that traps and transports pollen.

The bee's abdomen is the squishy part where the intestines are located. If she is a worker honeybee, she also has a special stomach, called a crop, where nectar begins the process of turning into honey. At the end of a female bee's abdomen is a stinger. She will use this to defend herself and her nest. It is a common misconception that all bees die when they sting. Only one species, the honeybee,

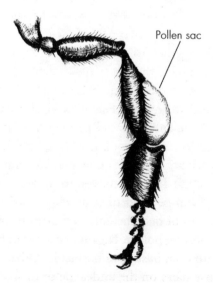

Pollen sac

Honeybee pollen sac

Honeybee sting   Bumblebee sting

Stings

has a barbed sting, like a fishing hook, that gets lodged in the skin of the assailant and rips the bee's body apart as she pulls away. Females of other bee species have a needle-like stinger that they can retract and use again.

Generally, if left alone bees are docile insects. A few species are stingless but have developed strong, powerful mandibles for biting intruders to their nest, and some can also excrete acid. Male bees cannot sting, because they have a sexual organ where the stinger should be. Mating is the sole reason for the males' existence, and once they have passed on their genes, they serve little purpose and don't live much longer. For this reason, most of the bees you will see foraging on flowers are females.

Astonishingly, bee mothers can decide whether the egg they lay will develop into a male or female. When the egg is laid, she decides whether or not sperm will be released from her spermatheca (the sac where she stores sperm after mating). Fertilized eggs develop into female bees, and unfertilized eggs develop into males. This system is called haplodiploidy: male bees are haploid, containing

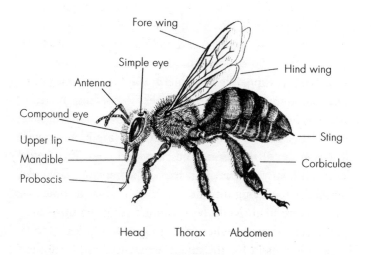

Fore wing

Simple eye

Hind wing

Antenna

Compound eye

Upper lip — Sting

Mandible

Proboscis — Corbiculae

Head   Thorax   Abdomen

Honeybee worker

only genetic material from their mother, while females are diploid, containing genetic material from both their mother and father.

Carl Linnaeus, the eighteenth-century father of modern taxonomy, came up with the idea of classing every organism by genus and species. The first bee he described was the honeybee, *Apis mellifera*: of the genus *Apis* (Latin for bee) and the species *mellifera* (Greek for honey-bearing), but nowadays this is the scientific name used for a specific honeybee species that originated in Europe, the Western honeybee.

Since that first scientific bee name, whenever a new type of bee is recorded, it is given an official genus and species name in Latin or Greek. These names help to avoid confusion, because common names for the same bee often differ from country to country. Each genus, such as *Apis*, and *Bombus*, the bumblebees, has also been placed into one of seven main bee families according to shared characteristics or behaviour. All the different honeybee and bumblebee species belong to the Apidae family, along with flower bees *(Anthophora)* and carpenter bees *(Xylocopa)*. They all transport pollen in baskets known as corbiculae on their back legs.

Little and large

The world's largest bee is the *Megachile pluto*, or Wallace's giant bee, named after the Victorian naturalist, Alfred Russel Wallace, who first recorded it. It measures 4cm (1.6in) long with a gigantic 6.3cm (2.5in) wingspan and has jaws like a stag beetle. It had not been seen for thirty-eight years and was feared extinct until its rediscovery in 2019 on an Indonesian island, nesting inside an active arboreal termite mound. In contrast, the tiniest bees are less than 2mm (0.08in) long and are members of the *Euryglossina (Quasihesma)* group native to Australia.

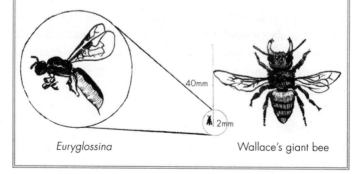

40mm

2mm

Euryglossina   Wallace's giant bee

✦ Bumblebees ✦

Most people, when they hear the word 'bee', probably think of the plump, boldly striped bumblebee. Its size, dense fur, striking markings and leisurely gait among flowers make it a handsome, friendly-looking creature and a favourite of illustrators of children's books.

So it may come as a surprise to learn that bumblebees account for only 1 per cent of bee species worldwide – and that they don't make the honey we eat.

Bumblebees all share the name *Bombus*, derived from the Latin word for buzzing. The 250 different species are found mainly in the northern hemisphere, since their larger size and furry coats equip them to forage in low temperatures. They are thought to have originated 30–40 million years ago in central Asia, where many still reside, and to have spread from the Himalayas to Europe, China and even north of the Arctic Circle. Around 20 million years ago, they crossed to North America, and a handful of species made it down to South America, the only part of the southern hemisphere where they are native.

Until the 1920s, the bumblebee's common English name was humble-bee. The word occurs in William Shakespeare's *A Midsummer Night's Dream* (1595–6) and in Charles Darwin's *On the Origin of Species* (1859). Even the first proper book devoted to bumblebees,

Bumblebee

published in 1912, was called *The Humble-bee; its life history and how to domesticate it*, by Frederick Sladen. Beatrix Potter's *Tale of Miss Tittlemouse* (1910) is thought to include one of the first mentions of a bumblebee, in the character Queen Babbitty Bumble, who makes her nest of moss in the old storeroom where the house-proud mouse hoards her nuts.

The name has stuck, probably because it so aptly describes the way these rotund bees 'bumble' endearingly and awkwardly around the flowers. Their body shape appears to defy the laws of aerodynamics – so much so that many have questioned how they actually manage to fly. But fly they can, despite their large bodies and heavy loads. So how do they do it? The answer seems to be a mixture of technique and brute force. With some clever biological engineering, the wings of a bumblebee beat at 200 beats per minute, but rather than up and down, the sweep is more from front to back. This motion creates tiny swirling masses of air, like tiny tornadoes, with low pressure at the centre. When the lower-pressure vortices are kept above the wings, the higher pressure below keeps the bee airborne. Thanks to this, and strong muscles that twist and turn the wings, the bees are capable of very delicate flying manoeuvres.

✦ Social bees ✦

Bumblebees, like honeybees, are among the social bees that live together in a colony with a queen, many worker bees and a few males. But they never make more than a few grams of honey, because bumblebee colonies die at the end of each summer, so there is no need for them to build up a store for winter. In contrast, honeybee colonies survive all year round, so they make vast quantities of honey to give the bees energy when it's cold and there is little to eat outside the nest.

Although the bumblebee colony is annual, young queen bees do live through the winter in a dormant state, surviving on their fat reserves. Like the groundhog and the dormouse, they emerge in early spring from a small hole underground, or from under a pile of leaves.

When the ground is still covered in frost, the large bumblebee queens can be seen buzzing around a scarce patch of snowdrops or crocuses, or higher up in the catkins of the pussy willow tree.

Bumblebees are among the first bees to appear each year because they have special adaptations that allow them to withstand blustery showers and chilly winds. As well as having a thick and insulating coat, they can also generate internal heat by shivering their flight muscles without flapping their wings. Those muscle contractions can make them much warmer than the surrounding environment, but they require a lot of energy. They cannot take off and fly unless their body temperature is at least

Queen buff-tailed bumblebee with crocuses

27°C (80°F), so they need to eat almost constantly to keep warm. A bumblebee is only ever about forty minutes from starvation; if she runs out of energy she can no longer fly to the flowers to get her energy drink. If you see a stationary bumblebee queen on a flower or on the ground in spring, you can help her by giving her a drop of sugary water to power up her muscles.

Among the earliest bees to appear each year are the common buff-tailed bumblebee (*Bombus terrestris*) queens, identifiable by their 20mm-length bodies and light-coloured bottoms. They can be heard buzzing around hazel, alder and pussy willow trees, where the drooping catkins provide an excellent early source of the protein-rich pollen they need to help their eggs to develop. They have sperm stored in their bodies from mating the previous summer, and once their eggs are mature, they can start producing a new colony.

Out on a brisk spring walk in the countryside, if you look down you might see a buff-tailed bumblebee queen zigzagging in the undergrowth. She is looking for a new nest – an empty mouse hole, for example, would be ideal. When she finds a promising subterranean space, she will crawl inside and determine if it's the right size to bring up her family. If she is lucky, it will already be stocked with insulation material such as moss, grass or fur.

In urban locations, bumblebees may choose to build their nest under a garden shed, patio – or even in a crack in a paving stone, as we discovered one summer when we came home to find them zipping in and out of a small opening in the pavement outside our house.

Different species of bumblebee have different nesting requirements. The common carder bee (*Bombus pascuorum*), a small, brown bumblebee that gets its name from an archaic word meaning 'to tease out fibres', likes to nest just above ground and can sometimes be found in a

Common carder bee

pile of old leaves with nesting material it has 'carded' from plants using the bristles on its back legs.

Early bumblebees (*Bombus pratorum*) – recognizable by their attractive bright yellow bands and red bottoms – have been found nesting in lawnmowers and buckets, while red-tailed bumblebees (*Bombus lapidarius*) will sometimes nest in bird boxes, but not until the chicks have fledged. Tree bumblebees (*Bombus hypnorum*), as their name suggests, also nest high up, and these black, white and ginger bees can often be seen buzzing around empty bird boxes they have moved into. In North America, the orange-rumped, or black-tailed, bumblebee (*Bombus melanopygus*), is commonly found in attics.

Each bumblebee queen has to find a separate home. Her mate died last summer, so at this stage in her life she is a single mum nesting alone, like most of the 25,000 bee species. But unlike the solitary bees, she is preparing her home to raise a colony of bees that will live together as a community.

✦ Annual life cycle ✦

After a female bumblebee has found a suitable location for her nest and rearranged the furniture to create a snug cavity, she makes a structure out of the wax that she secretes from a gland in her body. She mixes the wax (which is converted from some of the sugar in nectar) with pollen and uses her mouth parts to knead the substance into a thimble-shaped structure called a honeypot. In it she will store regurgitated nectar mixed with saliva that creates a form of honey. She needs this energy drink to power her muscles and shiver her body when she is incubating her eggs to keep them at 30°C (86°F), much like a bird clutching her eggs.

Some bumblebee species make a second wax pot in which to store pollen and lay their eggs. Others roll the pollen into a small pea-sized ball and coat it in wax. They then make a small hole in the middle of the ball and push their first batch of sixteen tiny sausage-like eggs into it.

After about four days, the eggs hatch into larvae and start to eat the pollen. At this point, the queen becomes a doting mother, busy foraging for food from early morning until it starts to get dark to feed her hungry brood, and using wax to extend the nursery so each larvae has space to grow. They are totally dependent on the pollen she brings them, so the key to successfully raising her first brood is the ready availability and proximity of early sources of pollen.

After gorging themselves until they can grow no fatter, the larvae spin a cocoon using silk from glands in their mouth. Inside the cocoon they begin the extraordinary transformation into an adult bumblebee.

After two weeks the adult bees emerge, biting their way out of the cocoon. They are fully formed, except for their stripy coats which take a few days to develop. These newborns are all daughters who will take over foraging, nest building and guarding duties from their mother. This is the early social phase of the colony, as labour is divided between worker daughters and their mother. The queen will by now have laid a second batch of eggs, and these need to be fed by the workers.

On their first foraging trips, the new worker bees circle around the nest. They are making exploratory trips, looping back and forth to get their bearings and learn the route home. They are making a mental note of any salient features, such as large buildings and trees, and mapping it out to aid their return journey. Soon they will be able to take a much more direct path – a beeline, in fact. Once they are near the nest, they can smell their queen and sisters' distinctive pheromones.

Studies have shown bumblebees can travel at up to 25km/h (15.5mph). How far they will forage depends on the species and the availability of food. Common carder bee workers will fly up to 450m (492 yards) from the nest, whereas buff-tailed bumblebee workers will travel at least 750m (820 yards). Bumblebee colonies whose workers can fly further obviously have a better chance of survival when food is scarce and this could explain why buff-tailed bumblebees are the most common species.

From midsummer, the workers are the only bumblebees out foraging because the queen is at home laying more eggs. If the weather is dry and there is plenty of food coming in, the queen will lay many batches of eggs and the colony will rapidly expand to several hundred sisters and their mother. The buff-tailed and the North American common eastern bumblebee (*Bombus impatiens*) can have large families of up to 500 bees, while the colony of the early bumblebee is much smaller, typically containing around 200 workers.

Bumblebee nests are surprisingly messy and haphazard-looking clumps of misshapen wax pots. The round, ramshackle structures have been compared to deflated footballs and bear no resemblance to the architecturally precise hexagonal wax combs made by honeybees and some stingless bees (see page 50).

There comes a point, usually towards the end of the summer, when the queen needs to think about starting a new colony. Now she switches from producing female workers to producing males and new queens instead. It is thought that she releases a special pheromone to ensure that her larvae develop into worker bees. If she stops releasing this chemical, the fertilized eggs grow into new queens. The unfertilized eggs she lays produce male bees. When the new queens and males emerge from the nest, they are on a mission to find a mate.

✦ Boy bumblebees ✦

Male bumblebees can often be seen in late summer, hanging out together on patches of flowers drinking nectar, or patrolling an area waiting for the virgin queens. They are smaller and slimmer than the females, and sometimes have brighter coats. Some are a completely different colour, like the red-tailed bumblebee: the females, with their black bodies and striking red bottoms, are easy to spot, while the males have yellow hairs on their head and thorax and a paler backside. Generally, the purpose of the males is to mate, not to collect food, so they don't carry pollen on their bag legs. Neither do they sting, as they have an endophallus, a penis-like instrument for injecting sperm, instead of a stinger. This makes them harmless, even when, as tree bumblebee males sometimes do, they are buzzing boisterously around the entrance of a bird box in their hundreds in search of females.

Some North American species of bumblebee whose

mating rituals have been studied – including the red-belted *(Bombus refocinctus),* brown-belted *(Bombus griseocollis)* and Nevada *(Bombus nevadensis)* bumblebees – find a lookout post early in the morning that they aggressively defend against other males, and they wait there, sometimes for days on end, marking the post with pheromones to attract the opposite sex.

When they arrive, the male will grab the virgin queen from behind, often in flight, and try to copulate with her. Her larger size means she is able to shake off any unsuitable admirer. She only mates once (unlike honeybees, see page 56), so wants to ensure that the father of her children is strong, healthy and attractive. In contrast, male bumblebees mate many times. Their sole purpose is to spread the colony's genes. The male grips a willing virgin with his powerful claspers at the end of his abdomen and inserts his endophallus. After he's deposited his sperm, he also releases a sticky substance that forms a plug to prevent her from mating again.

Mating season varies across bumblebee species. The early bumblebee, for example, mates early in midsummer, while common carder bees are one of the last to do so, at the end of the summer. The newly mated queens hibernate soon after mating, even if the weather's still warm and the flowers are in full bloom. Before they begin their long sleep they need to build up their body fat by drinking nectar from many flowers.

Back at the old colony, the workers will have died off and the original queen will be fading. You may find one of these old, weary bumblebees on a flower in late summer, incapable of flight. She will be on her last journey. A drop of sugary water won't help her now because her colony is coming to its natural end. But she has accomplished what nature intended. She has successfully reared one colony and bred new males and queens who will rear further colonies next year. What's more, in the process these bees have pollinated a plethora of flowering plants that have produced fruits, nuts and seeds for birds and other wildlife, and food for us, too.

⋆ 'Bee-loud glade' ⋆

One of the best ways to observe different types of bumblebee at close range is to plant large clumps of foxgloves. By midsummer, the stately spires are bumblebee magnets. Their stems covered in big, bell-shaped flowers with a large landing lip, are the perfect draw.

A strategically placed bench will allow bumblebee admirers to sit and watch the bees endearingly going about their daily business collecting nectar and pollen. Sitting very still, surrounded by towering foxgloves and buzzing bees, it will feel as though you have created Yeats' 'bee-loud glade', even in a small backyard.

Garden bumblebee

You are likely to see the chubby garden bumblebee (*Bombus hortorum*). Her 15mm (0.6in)-long tongue is almost the length of her rotund body, allowing her to access the deeply hidden nectar more easily than other bumblebees. She is recognizable by the black skullcap pattern on her yellow thorax. And she'll often fly from flower to flower – looking more like she is bouncing as she dips and rises – with her tongue extended ready for the next gulp. It's delightful to watch.

In contrast, the smaller common carder bee, with a shorter tongue, has to squeeze herself right inside the flower head to have any chance of a drink. She may emerge a few minutes later, made unrecognizable with a dusting of pollen over her brown coat, as the flower intended. It's a comical sight.

If you look closely at the large foxglove petals, you may see some of them have holes at the base. This is evidence of nectar robbing. Despite the co-dependency between bees and flowers, some short-tongued bumblebee species manage to steal a flower's nectar by making a small insertion in the petal near to the liquid and then stick their short tongues through it to suck up the fluid. They don't have long enough tongues to reach into the flowers' deep nectar reservoirs and they cheat the flower because they are not pollinating it. Short-tongued buff-tailed bumblebees are the likely culprits. Their nefarious actions will likely attract other short-tongued bees, including tree bumblebees and red-tailed bumblebees, as well as honeybees who can reuse the hole. It appears that nectar robbing is more likely if there aren't enough suitable open, daisy-like flowers nearby that have easily accessible nectar for short-tongued bees.

Nectar robber

✦ Predators ✦

The female bumblebees are equipped with a sting and will use it if their nest is threatened. But those in our garden always seem very docile when they are out foraging.

A bumblebee will give you a warning sign if she feels you are getting too close. She raises her forelegs to say 'back off'. It may look like she's waving, but it's meant to be intimidating and it means that it's time to step away.

Bumblebees' bold-coloured stripes act as a signal to warn predators that they could get stung if they try to eat them. Even the males have stripy uniforms to deceive predators into thinking they will harm them.

Badgers, mink and skunks are all capable of tearing bumblebee nests to shreds, but one of the bees' major predators is the inconspicuous wax moth.

Warning sign

Wax moth

They lay their eggs in bee nests and their caterpillars eat everything – grubs, wax, honey, pollen, even adult bees – and the bumblebees seem incapable of fighting back. As a result, few of the bumblebee nests started in the spring actually succeed in rearing large, healthy colonies. This high failure rate explains why a colony has to produce so many queens. Furthermore, some healthy colonies may actually contain cuckoo species. Like cuckoo birds, there are bumblebees that don't make their own nest but sneak into the ready-made home of the host species (one of a similar size and pattern), kill the queen and make slaves of her daughters by emitting a strong pheromone that tricks the workers into obeying the imposter. The cuckoo queen only produces males and new queens, but no workers, as she exploits the resident daughters, who are forced to forage for the cuckoo bee's family.

Of the twenty-four bumblebee species in Britain, six are cuckoos, of which the most widespread is the forest cuckoo bumblebee (*Bombus sylvestris*), a parasite of the early bumblebee. In North America, the aptly named indiscriminate cuckoo bumblebee (*Bombus insularis*), will occupy the home of seven or more host species.

Forest cuckoo bumblebee

✦ Bumblebee species ✦

There are 250 bumblebee species worldwide. The seven species that visit our city garden are widespread across much of Europe and Asia.

North America's forty-six native bumblebee species come in many hues and tones. Among the most eye-catching are the tri-coloured bumblebee (*Bombus ternarius*) with her orange jacket, yellow body and black head and tail, and Hunt's bumblebee (*Bombus Huntii*) with her wide band of orange. The most widespread bumblebee in the eastern United States is the common eastern bumblebee (*Bombus impatiens*), which has a cropped yellow jacket over her black body. On the west side, the two-form, or black-notched, bumblebee (*Bombus bifarius*) is more abundant.

Of the sixty-eight European bumblebees, the continent's largest, *Bombus fragrans* – native to the steppes of Ukraine and Russia – is one of the more unusual-looking bumblebees. The female has a thin black vertical stripe down the middle of her furry, orange, elongated abdomen. The remaining bumblebee species are spread across the colder regions of Asia, including the Qinghai-Tibet Plateau in China, where more species live than anywhere else in the world. A handful are also found in South America.

The most northerly bee is the Arctic bumblebee

(*Bombus polaris*) who lives in the far northern reaches of Alaska, Canada, Scandinavia and Russia. She can withstand the freezing temperatures because she is large, and the heat she generates by shivering her large flight muscles is trapped by her extra-thick coat. On sunny days, queens and workers have been seen sitting inside Arctic poppies. The flowers act like a magnifying glass and concentrate the rays of the sun to warm up the bees.

Arctic bumblebee on poppies

Biggest bumblebee

The largest bumblebee in the world is the giant golden bumblebee (*Bombus dahlbomii*). One of the few South American bumblebees, it lives in high altitudes in the Andes and thanks to its size – queens can measure up to 40mm (1.6in) – it is often called the flying mouse (see page 152).

Giant golden bumblebee

✦ Honeybees ✦

In contrast to small bumblebee colonies, honeybees live in highly structured social hierarchies of tens of thousands of bees. Each colony contains as many as 50,000 bees separated into three castes: workers, drones and a queen. The vast majority are infertile workers, a few hundred are male drones, and there is one fertile queen bee who is their mother.

These are all component parts of a system that entomologists call a superorganism. We like to use the analogy of a tree to explain how a honeybee colony works. A tree is made up of roots, the trunk, bark, branches, leaves, and sometimes blossom. All these parts work together and make up the tree.

People are often upset to learn that an individual worker bee may live for as little as six weeks in the summer, but if we view her like the leaf of a tree, it feels less sad. When we see a green leaf on a tree, we understand that it's a small part of a bigger picture. It's the same with honeybees. The slender, striped honeybee we see flying around the flowers is not an individual animal but one small part of a larger system.

If you remove one leaf from a tree, the leaf dies but the tree continues. The same applies to our individual honeybee visiting a flower. Take her away from her colony

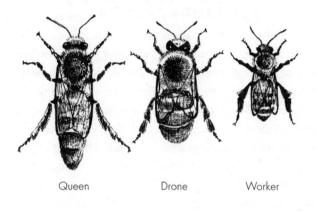

Queen   Drone   Worker

Honeybee castes

and she will die, but the colony continues. The leaf and the honeybee also play a similar role as food and energy collectors. The tree gets food through photosynthesis, the process by which leaves turn sunlight into sugar, while the honeybee colony gets its food and sugars from the pollen and nectar that its workers collect. Later in the year, the leaves fall from a deciduous tree – in a show of autumnal splendour – because the tree isn't doing much growing in the cold winter months, so there is little need for energy collectors.

Similarly, the honeybee colony doesn't grow in the cold winter months, so most of the energy collectors – the worker bees – die without being replaced: the queen stops laying eggs and the colony shrinks to around 10,000 bees. Both the colony and the tree enter a state of minimal activity, holding out until spring when the growing season returns.

Now the cycle begins again. The tree grows new leaves, the honeybee queen produces new worker bees, and the systems revert to their energy-collecting ways in earnest.

The tree's flowers contain male and female parts that, once fertilized, produce seeds that can grow into a new tree. Likewise, a honeybee colony has male and female parts – male bees, called drones, and a fertile queen who, once mated, will create a new honeybee colony.

Our analogy has extra resonance because both systems are so reliant on each other. The tree needs the bees for their pollination services, and the bee colony needs a flowering tree to feed its thousands of hungry mouths. In fact, honeybees aren't seen foraging on garden flowers as frequently as bumblebees or solitary bees, because they are often high above our heads in a tree.

In the wild, the honeybee colony actually lives in a hollow cavity of a tree. Inside the dark trunk, worker bees construct sheets of honeycomb from scales of wax excreted from eight glands on the underside of their abdomen. Using their mouthparts and legs, they manipulate the scales into the most amazing, intricate, uniform and mesmerizing sheets of double-sided hexagonal cells with between 5,000–8,000 cells per sheet. They build each sheet from the top down, curving and winding them around each

Horse chestnut tree flowers

other in a wonderful organic wavy shape, and leaving just enough space between them for the two-way traffic of bees. The six-sided cell structure is regarded as the pinnacle of engineering in nature. It led Charles Darwin to note: 'Beyond this stage of perfection in architecture, natural selection could not lead.'

The comb forms the backbone of the colony, providing a nursery, where the queen lays eggs that develop into larvae and metamorphose into adult bees; a larder, where the workers store the winter food; and even a dance floor, where important announcements are made. Bees can communicate by vibrating their bodies while holding on to the comb. This transmits a message around their home.

The queen bee can lay up to 2,000 eggs every day in late spring and summer. The workers take twenty-one days to develop into adult bees, the drones, twenty-four days. The worker bee emerges as a fully grown adult, slightly fluffy and weak. She spends the first three weeks of her life inside the dark nest, maturing. In that time, she feeds the hungry larvae who, unlike caterpillars, don't have legs. Newborn workers also clean and prepare cells for the next egg. As the worker matures, she develops her sting and her poison gland to be ready to defend the nest.

Once they have reached maturity, worker bees become energy collectors, flying to fetch nectar. The workers also collect pollen for the larvae to eat, water to cool down the hive, and propolis – a sticky antibacterial resin exuded

Daily commute

Imagine carrying pollen and nectar that can weigh more than half your own body weight. It would be tiring work. It's estimated that a worker honeybee can fly over 800km (500 miles) before she succumbs to muscle fatigue and as a result she often dies on the wing. That distance usually takes twenty days in the summer, which means she flies on average 40km (25 miles) a day. Since she flies around 20km (12 miles) per hour, her daily commute takes about two hours. Even if she works closer to home to be more energy efficient, she will still fly for a total of two hours a day, but broken up into shorter flights of about twenty-six minutes.

by some trees – to seal any holes in their nest. They map the location of their hive, using notable features on the landscape, to find their way home.

◆ Making honey ◆

Turning nectar into honey is a two-stage process of chemically changing the sugars in the nectar from complex into simple sugars and then reducing the water content of the liquid down to 20 per cent or less. When the bee drinks the nectar, it goes into her special honey stomach, which contains an enzyme that breaks sucrose down into fructose and glucose. On returning to the nest, the foraging worker passes this liquid to a house bee, who drops it into the cells of the comb and then uses its wings to pass a warm air current over the liquid to draw the water off. The bees also use their mouthparts to churn the nectar, which further helps to convert the sugars and aids evaporation. When this is done, the cells in which the honey is stored are sealed with a white wax cap. This keeps the honey fresh in an airtight container for the winter. The honeybee colony has evolved to survive when it's cold and there's little to eat outside. The bees don't fly when the thermometer drops below about 13°C (55°F), or in rain, or strong winds. The population reduces to 10,000 or so worker bees and the queen. They huddle together like penguins on ice caps, and shiver their flight muscles to keep themselves and their home warm. They derive the energy for this from their store of honey. This winter survival is unique to bees that make honey.

Busy, busy bees

- On one flight, a foraging honeybee can visit 200–300 flowers and collect 0.05g (0.002oz) of nectar.

- In one day, she can visit up to 2,000 flowers and collect 0.5g (0.02oz) of nectar.

- In five days, 10,000–20,000 foragers can bring in 5kg of nectar to the hive for the bees to turn into 1.5kg (3.3lbs) of honey.

- It takes 12,000 bee hours to make 1.5kg of honey.

Cranebill with honeybee

✦ Continuing the generations ✦

The honeybee colony has an amazing method of procreation. The colony splits in two, with the old queen and half the colony leaving to find a new home. This process is called swarming. They leave behind new queens, one of whom will mate and create a new colony of bees in the existing home.

The pregnancy starts after the workers have made twenty or so acorn-like cells that hang down vertically from the comb. Then they direct the queen to lay an egg in each one. Once the eggs are hatched in these special new queen cells, the larvae are fed a special protein-rich substance called royal jelly, made from glands within the worker bee's head. This highly nutritious food miraculously changes the developing larvae into queen bees rather than workers.

While the queen larvae are growing, the colony is also preparing the old queen for an imminent flight by putting her on a strict diet so that she is able to fly. Half the workers in the colony gorge themselves on three days' worth of honey to give them the energy to accompany her to a new nesting site – and a reserve of sugar to start building new comb.

When the queen larvae enter the pupal stage and spin their cocoons, the colony is ready to split. The sight of 20,000 or so worker bees and the old queen leaving the nest to take up residence elsewhere can look rather alarming, but it is a fascinating spectacle. They pour out of the entrance of the nest and blanket the surrounding area, waiting for the queen to come to a stop. Once she does, some of the workers surround her and send out a strong pheromone from Nasonov glands at the end of their abdomens to say, 'This is where the queen is. Come and find her.' The 20,000-strong swarm pick up this scent, and within minutes come together around the queen. This oval-shaped cluster may hang off a tree branch with the queen somewhere in the centre. In an urban location they may gather somewhere less convenient, such as a traffic light, or the side of a building in a busy high street. There they wait until they get a signal from the scout bees who have been out searching for a new nest. Different scouts have looked at a number of options, and they check out each other's sites to make a collective decision about which is more suitable. They then return to the cluster of bees and dance excitedly until it flies away in the direction of the chosen new home. When the bees arrive, they immediately begin to build wax comb so that the queen can start to lay eggs and expand the colony.

Back at the original home, the young developing queens take eight more days to emerge. But a colony can only have one queen, so only one will survive. When the royal ladies appear there is a fight to the death, the sole survivor of which becomes the new queen. This is the colony's way of making sure the fittest queen is selected to produce a new colony.

A few days later, weather permitting, the victorious virgin leaves the nest and goes on her nuptial flight to a mating congregation area in the sky that is frequented by numerous drones from the surrounding district. While bumblebee queens and female solitary bees mate only once, the honeybee queen mates with a dozen or more drones on her nuptial flight before returning to her nest. She now has the sperm she needs for the next four to five years in her special sperm sac. She will start to lay fertilized eggs, and twenty-one days later the adult workers of the next generation will be born. Workers all have the same mum but multiple paternal lines mean the colony consists of full sisters and half-sisters. This genetic diversity allows for workers with slightly different characteristics, which is thought to make the colony better able to fight infection or adapt to environmental challenges.

The queen honeybee only leaves the nest twice in her life, to mate and to swarm. She is unlikely to be seen by a casual observer on either occasion as she is always surrounded by an entourage who control her every movement. Unlike a bumblebee queen, she is never alone in searching for a new nest or foraging for nectar and pollen to feed her young. The colony's worker bees do everything she and the colony requires. In fact, far from being a mighty sovereign, the queen honeybee is an egg-laying slave to her colony, fed by the workers when the colony wants more eggs laid, starved when it needs fewer.

✦ Drones ✦

The role of the male honeybee is purely to spread a colony's genes. They are nothing more than flying sperm carriers. They do no household chores, nor do they collect food for their mother or sisters. A few thousand drones are produced by the colony in late spring to mate with virgin queens. Only the strongest and most virile are successful. As they pull away after copulation they die because their sexual organs are attached to the queen and their body is ripped apart – in much the same way as honeybee workers after stinging. This is nature's way of saying, 'You have played your part and are now surplus to requirements.' Drones who don't manage to mate are kicked out of the nest by their sisters at the end of the summer and left to die.

✦ Alarm signal ✦

The only time a queen will need her sting is at the beginning of her adult life, when she uses it to kill her rival queens in the hive. Her sting is needle-like and can be inserted and retracted many times without causing her any damage, unlike her self-sacrificing workers.

Charles Darwin was intrigued by the way that female worker bees die without passing on their genes, as it seemed to contradict his theory of natural selection. If an individual devoted her life to her colony without ever reproducing, how could she pass on her genes? It wasn't until he realized that the worker bee was only a part of the whole living organism and her death in the act of stinging helped to keep the colony as a whole alive that things began to make sense.

The worker's sting is ingenious for the defence of the colony because its poison sack produces a chemical called the alarm pheromone. This smell attracts other worker bees to the sting and signals for them to attack the assailant. Imagine that a large bear is stealing honey from a bees' nest. If a lone worker bee stings the bear on the nose, it will most likely not be enough to deter the bear. But because the alarm attracts more workers, the bear receives multiple stings, enough to force it to retreat, especially as the sting has a pump that continues to inject the venom from the poison sac into the intruder even after the honeybee has pulled away.

Chemical pheromones are one of the colony's principal means of communication. The queen, for example, has her own distinct pheromone that lets the other bees know she is highly fertile. When the intensity of this pheromone wanes, it signals that she is less fecund and probably dying. This acts as a trigger for the colony to replace her. As we have seen, bees also communicate in their dark cavity by vibrating their bodies on the wax comb. They also have a third, rather more sophisticated means of imparting information.

⋆ Hive talking ⋆

Honeybees also have a unique way of giving directions. When they need to communicate the location of a food source to a co-worker, the honeybee stages a performance: the waggle dance. Inside the darkness of the nest, she shakes and vibrates, signalling that she has news. Her vibrations ripple along the honeycomb dance floor, alerting potential foragers. Then she begins to spin around in a figure of eight over and over again; turning around to the right, to complete one circle, then turning to the left, to complete another. As she performs the straight line part of the dance, she waggles her abdomen.

The dance tells her audience the distance and direction of the food. It is truly remarkable that this tiny creature

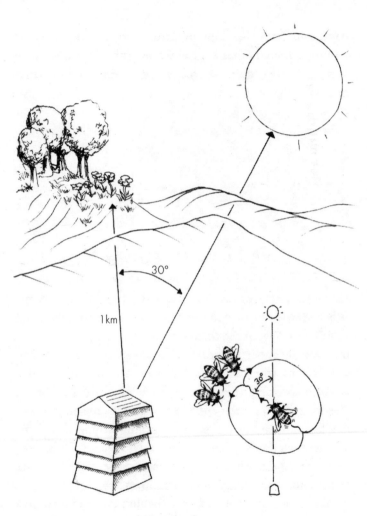

Waggle dance

can convey such complex information about food that could be more than 5km (3 miles) away. If she dances with her head pointing upwards on the comb, this says, 'Come out of the entrance, find the position of the sun and fly towards it.' If she dances with her head pointing down the honeycomb, the recruited workers leave the hive, find the sun and turn around and fly away from it. If the worker dances with her head pointing to the right, this shows the source is to the right of the direction of the sun. If she waggles for half a second, the bees know to fly 500m (547 yards). If she waggles for a whole second, they will need to fly twice that far. Now the bees know both which way and how far to fly. Before they leave the hive, they will remember the particular smell of the flora on the dancing bee and when they reach the vicinity they will smell their way to the exact flowers.

When the new recruits return loaded down with booty, they will repeat the dance to recruit more foragers. At any one moment there may be any number of bees dancing in different directions across the dance floor, vying for attention. The more bees that are dancing the same dance, smelling of the same flower, the more foragers that food source will attract.

Scout honeybees also use the waggle dance during swarming, when they are looking for a new home.

Communicating abstract ideas about faraway locations of food is not common among animals who usually rely

Karl von Frisch

In the 1950s, Austrian ethologist (ethology is the scientific study of animal behaviour) Dr Karl von Frisch published *The Dancing Bees*, an account of the life and senses of the honeybee. Von Frisch described the discovery of the honeybees' language, the way that they move on the comb inside the hive to communicate the location of a food source. It was he who first called this movement a dance, and it became known as the 'waggle dance'.

Though the 'dance' of the bees had been observed by beekeepers, the significance of the bees' movement only came to light after von Frisch's extensive research.

By placing markers on bees who had been feeding at feeding stations set up by researchers and then observing their movements in the hive, von Frisch saw that the bees' dance changed when the feeding station was moved to a different position.

For this discovery, among others, von Frisch was awarded the Nobel Prize in Physiology or Medicine in 1973.

on smell or sight. A dog, for example, can't communicate to another dog with a bark that says, 'If you walk in a straight line towards that tree for about twenty minutes you'll find a bone.'

✦ Honeybee species ✦

There are about a dozen honeybee species worldwide. The most widespread is the 14mm (0.6in)-long western honeybee (*Apis mellifera*). It evolved in Africa and Europe 35 million years ago and has been transported around the globe by humans for hundreds, if not thousands, of years to pollinate crops and make honey. There are many subspecies of western honeybees, each with slightly different characteristics. The Italian western honeybee (*Apis mellifera linguistica*) is a light-coloured, highly productive and docile bee. In contrast, the black western honeybee (*Apis mellfiera mellifera*) is a darker, less productive and more defensive bee, native to northern Europe.

The Africanized honeybee, better known as the infamous 'killer' bee, is a highly defensive hybrid of western honeybee subspecies that originated in Africa *(Apis mellifera scutellata)* and several are native to Europe. Cross-bred by scientists in

Brazil in the 1950s, they escaped the laboratory and spread northwards through Central America as far as the southern states of the USA, where their propensity to swarm and to sting in large numbers and with little provocation has, unsurprisingly, caused alarm.

The eastern honeybee (*Apis cerana*) lives in India, Japan, China, Korea and South East Asia. It is slightly smaller than the western honeybee, but lives much the same way as its European cousin and is kept by humans in hives for honey production and pollination. Two dwarf honeybee species (*Apis florea* and *Apis andreniformis*) also live in hot parts of Asia and nest outside. They can be half the size of the western honeybee, at only 7mm (0.3in) long. They make a simple sheet of honeycomb wrapped around a branch of a tree, often in dense foliage to camouflage themselves from predators such as ants and spiders. They produce small colonies and make only small reserves of honey because there are rarely long periods of bad weather when they cannot go out to forage.

The giant honeybee (*Apis dorsata*) colony also lives outside on one large honeycomb sheet that can be a metre in height and more across. It hangs down from the underside of branches in the forests of South East Asia and China, from Thailand to the Philippines and Indonesia, where instead of winter and summer there are wet and dry seasons. The bees nest at high altitudes in the dry season and when the flora runs out, migrate to lower elevations, establishing new nests there for the mass flowering of the monsoon season. This journey can cover 200km (over 120 miles) and take a month or so, with the bees resting in large clusters, or bivouacs, in trees along the way.

The giant honeybee uses a fascinating method of defence known as shimmering, a display aimed at intimidating predatory wasps, birds, or mammals. When an enemy approaches, the bees line up along the surface of the nest and raise their abdomens in a sequential order in a spectacular Mexican wave.

Giant giant honeybee

Giant honeybees generally measure 20mm (0.8in) long, but the Himalayan giant honeybee, which is found in huge cliff-edge nests on the mountains of the Himalayas, is even bigger. The workers of a colony can reach 30mm (1.2in), making them the true giants of the honeybee world.

✦ Stingless bees ✦

Like all bees, stingless bees are incredibly efficient pollinators. And like the honeybees, they make honey as an energy source for times of nectar scarcity, or when inclement weather stops them foraging. They, too, live in an advanced social structure with a caste system of the queen, sterile female workers and male drones; their perennial colonies function as superorganisms.

There are some 500 documented species of stingless bee, most of which are tiny and black and live in the tropics of central and South America. A few other species are found in Asia, Africa and Australia, although there are likely more species to be discovered. The South American *Melipona* genus of stingless bee, locally called the *abeja criolla,* is well documented because the ancient Mayans began harvesting its honey thousands of years ago. Although stingless bees tend to be much less productive than honeybees, one of the *Tetragonula*, a group of stingless bees found in Australia, has a species tellingly called the sugarbag bee (*Tetragonula carbonaria*).

Stingless bees do in fact have a sting, but it is ineffectual.

Instead they have developed other ways to defend themselves. They have powerful mandibles that can give an intruder a nasty bite; some, like the *Oxytrigona* or fire bees, can excrete formic acid to irritate their assailants. They will attack in large numbers, finding their way into sensitive body parts such as the ear, nose, eyes and mouth.

Stingless bee nests have been found to vary greatly in size, containing just a few dozen to 100,000 or more workers, who are generally much smaller and darker than the western honeybee. They usually make their nests in a hollow tree trunk or a beetle burrow, but some species nest outdoors on tree branches or cliff faces. The nest is made from wax, resin and sometimes mud. It is visible because of the tube-like entrance that protrudes like the spout of a teapot. The bees also secrete wax to construct brood cells and food storage pots that resemble a bumblebee nest, although some species make amazing spirals from sheets of beeswax.

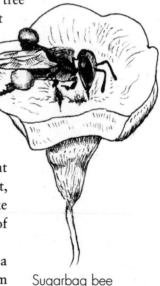

Sugarbag bee

When stingless bees start a new colony they don't swarm

like honeybees. Instead, half the workers transport building materials and food from the existing nest to a new site nearby. They go back and forth between the old and the new home like a removal van, but leave enough material behind for the new queen to raise a new colony after she has been on her nuptial flight.

Vulture bees

Three closely related species of stingless bee have abandoned flowers altogether. Members of the *Trigona* genus, found in Central America, are commonly called vulture bees because they appear to have developed a taste for carrion instead of flora and create a kind of honey from the dead and decaying flesh of animals. It just goes to show that there are exceptions to every rule in nature.

✦ Solitary bees ✦

Bee visitors to our small, urban back garden include a handful of different bumblebee species and many honeybees, we suspect from a hive a few streets away. But we also see less familiar bees. These are solitary bees, whose females nest alone. Although the vast majority of bees are of a solitary persuasion – there are 250 solitary bee species in the UK alone – they have been woefully overlooked. Some are not readily observed because of their diminutive size, others can easily be mistaken for flies, and a few look very similar to bumblebees or honeybees until you get really close and have a field guide to help identify them. Although solitary bees neither live in colonies nor make honey, they are every bit as important for the planet.

Glimpsing one of these unfamiliar bees provides a tingle of excitement. While busy foraging they are docile enough for us to get close and observe their distinct markings and idiosyncratic behaviour. We try to identify them with the help of photographs we've taken and Steven Falk's excellent *Field Guide to the Bees of Great Britain and Ireland* (2015). Once named, the visiting bee becomes a particular kind of bee, often with a beautifully evocative name: the hairy-footed flower bee (*Anthophora plumipes*), the red mason bee (*Osmia bicornis*), the leafcutter bee (*Megachile centuncularis*), the wool carder bee (*Anthidium*

Bee visiting lungwort

manicatum), the large-headed resin bee (*Heriades truncorum*), and the ivy mining bee (*Colletes hederae*).

Many of these bees feeding and nesting around our garden are common throughout the northern hemisphere. And once you become aware of them, it's as if a whole, hitherto invisible world has suddenly come into view.

◆ Hairy-footed flower bee ◆

The earliest solitary bee visitor of the year is the hairy-footed flower bee, whose orange-coloured hind legs are covered in feathery hairs right down to her titchy feet, which is where she gets her delightful name. North America, which is home to around 4,000 different bee species, has a similar flower bee.

There is something engaging about the way she darts and hovers among the delicate blue and white tubular flowers with her outstretched tongue – almost double the length of her body – and her legs tucked under her body, quite unlike how other bees fly. She will be picking up provisions from lungwort, dead nettles and comfrey, usually early in the morning, as she is dressed for cool weather in her thick black coat. It is not uncommon to think she is sitting motionless when she is actually shivering to warm herself up.

During her three-month life, she will nest alone in an existing small cavity in a wall, soft mortar, sometimes around a chimney stack, or in a burrow in clay soil. Although she lives by herself, she will often nest next door to other hairy-footed flower bees, as many solitary bees do. But these are neighbours rather than family. Some species, like the oak mining bee (*Andrena ferox*) and the big-headed mining bee (*Andrena bucephala*), even share a communal entrance to an extensive underground tunnelling system which branches out into individual rooms in which one egg is laid. Research suggests that these dense settlements, which can house hundreds of bees, are intended to provide safety in numbers. They're called aggregates, or villages,

Hairy-footed flower bee

Hairy-footed flower bee approaching a flower with her
tongue extended

but in an urban location a housing estate might be a more apt description.

Solitary bees forage close to home to conserve their energy. It's hard work, flying back and forth, sometimes carrying more than half their body weight in food, especially on cold days. It's often too wet or windy to forage, so they need to work quickly when the weather's fine.

Inside the nest, the bee divides up the space into separate rooms, or cells, and lines them with a waterproof substance secreted from a gland on her body. Each room will be provisioned with 'bee-bread' – a big blob of pollen and nectar mixed together. It takes many trips to fill one room with a substantial loaf, and on each trip she may visit hundreds of flowers. On top of each loaf, she lays an egg and when it hatches into a larva it will find itself lying on a bed of food.

Solitary bees lay female eggs towards the back of the nest, male eggs near the front. This is because male adult bees emerge a week or two earlier than the females. This gives them time to build up their strength for mating.

When the solitary bee has laid her final egg and sealed the nest, her maternal duties are done. The exhausted mum's muscles give up soon afterwards and she will die before her children are born. When her larvae appear, they gorge themselves on the bee-bread. They grow rapidly for six to eight weeks before spinning a silk cocoon and changing into a pupa. It is at this stage that they begin the transformation from ugly grub into handsome bee. This metamorphosis takes place over many months. Adult bees emerge the following spring, triggered by lengthening days and a slight rise in the temperature, to feed on the lungwort flowers, starting the whole cycle again.

Male hairy-footed flower bees, like all solitary bee males, are smaller than the female. They have a duller brown coat and were it not for the loud buzzing they make when hanging out in gangs on their favourite flowers, you might never notice them. When the jet black females arrive, they woo them with special pheromones. After mating, the female goes in search of a nest while the male seeks another partner.

There are some 450 different species of flower bee around the world. They include the green-eyed flower bee (*Anthophora bimaculata*) and the fork-tailed variety (*Anthophora furcate*).

٭ Master builders ٭

Solitary bees are classified into seven bee families usually according to the methods they use to construct their nests. The *Colletidae* family, for example, includes plasterer bees, so named because of the way they line their underground nests with the fine waterproof substance that they secrete. The *Andrenidae* are a large family of mining bees that excavate burrows underground, some with highly elaborate tunnelling systems, and are particularly common in temperate climates. The much rarer *Melittidae* are a smaller family of miners who visit particular flowers. The oldest known bee fossil is thought to be a species that belonged to the *Melittidae* 100 million years ago. Furrow bees dig nests in sand and soil and belong to the 4,000-strong *Halictidae* (sweat bee) family, which are found all over the world, including many in China. In contrast, there are just twenty mining bee species in the *Stenotritidae* family, found only in Australia.

Members of the cosmopolitan *Megachilidae* family have a much wider distribution and generally make their nest in existing, empty cavities such as plant stems, dead wood and old mortar. They include mason and leafcutter bees, who use their large jaws to fashion pieces of mud or leaves with which to partition and seal their nests. Other members of the family collect oils from certain plants to make their nests watertight, or tease out fibres from leaves to use as home furnishings.

Carpenter bees are arguably the most skilful solitary house builders. Their scientific name, *Xylocopa*, is Greek for woodcutter, because they are known for using their strong jaws to excavate a nest in anything wooden, from decaying tree stumps to man-made pallets or crates. Most

Violet carpenter bee

of the 730 species are tropical and subtropical, like the largest carpenter bee (*Xylocopa latipes*) with a 60mm (2.4in) wing span. Black all over, her metallic wings can glisten gold in the right light making her look magical, but the violet carpenter bee *(Xylocopa violacea*) is Europe's largest bee. Measuring up to 25mm (1in) long, she can appear quite intimidating. On our first encounter on a holiday in Italy, we kept our distance. But she flies slowly and, like most solitary bees, rarely stings. More recently, in Spain, we saw the same type of black-coloured bee foraging on rosemary, and noticed a beautiful violet sheen to her wings. Now that we had a name for her, and understood her temperament, we were better able to appreciate her beauty.

Carpenter bees, members of the *Apidae* family, carry pollen on their back legs. Pollen comes in a variety of colours, not just yellow. One of the many delights of observing bees is to see what colour pollen they are transporting and to try to work out which flower they have visited. But it is not as easy as it sounds – the colour of the grains bears no relation to the colour of the flowers. Oriental poppies, for example, have black pollen; yellow gorse produces reddish grains; and crocus pollen is orange.

Many of the bees who buzz around the blossoming apple tree at the bottom of our garden are carrying a load of orange pollen on their undersides, trapped in specially designed tufts of hair called scopa. This is one of the ways we can tell red mason bees from honeybees. The mason bee's 12mm (0.5in) body is also fractionally smaller, a little stouter, and has a much rounder bottom than a honeybee. The male red mason bee is a brownish colour: the red of their name refers to the colour of the female.

Scopa

Red mason bee

⁜ Cavity nesters ⁜

Mason bees naturally nest in small, dark cavities such as cracks in walls or hollow plant stems. To help them, we have attached a number of man-made nesting sites under the eaves of our shed. These 'bee hotels' are open-ended, cylindrical containers packed with 15cm (6in)-long hollow cardboard tubes of a diameter from 5mm–15mm (0.2–0.6in) (see page 169). Mason bees and leafcutter bees have checked in to the tubes to lay their eggs. The male red mason bees are the first to check out, the following spring. They chew their way out through the partition mud walls and their fuzzy heads and antennae can often be seen poking out of a tube, scouting out the terrain before they emerge. Once they have checked out, the males will buzz excitedly around the entrances for a week or so, waiting for the females to appear.

When the females finally emerge, there will be lots of activity as the quickest, strongest males try to seduce them. The male jumps on to the back of the bigger female and beats his wings to try to impress her. If she's not interested, she will shake him off. But if he meets her exacting standards, she will remain still while he thrusts from behind. Afterwards, her maternal instincts kick in and she flies off looking for a new nest. If we are lucky she will choose the clean, empty tubes in one of our bee hotels.

Mud is an important building material for red masons. If you leave an exposed piece of damp earth, you may see them collecting soil in their mandibles to take back to the nest. They chew and refashion this to build partition walls in the tubes, creating six or seven separate rooms. In each one of these they will provision pollen and nectar and lay an egg. Each female is capable of laying around thirty eggs, so she may need to commandeer four or five tubes. When each tube is full of eggs and pollen, the worn-out mum will plug the entrance with more mud and, like the hairy-footed flower bee a few months earlier, go off quietly to die. The following spring, her offspring will emerge to pollinate the apple tree and many other flowering plants.

By midsummer, the rose bushes look as if they have been attacked with a hole punch. In fact, the culprits are leafcutter bees who have been cutting out disc-shaped pieces of leaf with their scissor-like jaws. They are a bit darker in colour than honeybees and also have an orange scopa beneath their abdomen. But the easiest way to tell a leafcutter bee is when you spot one flying through the air carrying a leaf twice her size. It's an unforgettable sight as she clasps her load between her thighs, like a witch on her broomstick. Back at the nest, she will glue large pieces of leaf together with saliva to make the walls of the nursery. When she has laid all her eggs, she collects smaller pieces of leaves and chews them up into a paste

Leafcutter bee

to plug the entrances. It's not unusual for leafcutters and mason bees to nest next door to each other in a bee hotel and create green and brown front doors, sealed with mud or leaves.

In our garden, the patchwork leafcutter (*Megachile centuncularis*) is a regular visitor. In North America, it is the black and grey leafcutter (*Megachile melanophaea*) who is likely to be collecting rose leaves, while the alfalfa leafcutter (*Megachile rotundata*), employs alfalfa, clover or buckwheat for nest-building. Desert leafcutter bees cut holes in cactus flowers and take them home to use as wallpaper. North American leafcutters are likely to be living next door to blue orchard mason bees (*Osmia lignaria*) or blueberry mason bees (*Osmia ribifloris*).

⋆ How to tell them apart ⋆

Some solitary bees are named after their appearance rather than their homemaking skills. Male long-horned bees (*Eucera longicornis*), for example, have two outlandishly long antennae that extend their entire wingspan. The female pantaloon bee (*Dasypoda hirtipes*) looks as if she is wearing oversized orange trousers on her back legs. These are actually extra-large pollen baskets. They also help her to excavate a burrow in sand, and create a unique fan-shaped spoil heap to one side of the entrance that you might see when walking among coastal dunes.

The female tawny mining bee (*Andrena fulva*) is one of the most striking European solitary bees, with luscious, bright orange plumes on her thorax and abdomen. She nests underground, often alongside hundreds of others of her kind, in an elaborate burrow system with lateral

Pantaloon bee

tunnels radiating away from the shaft of the main burrow, and each ending in a single room where an egg will be laid. In spring, it is quite a spectacle seeing them tunnelling up through lawns, their fox-coloured coats clashing with the green grass. They spare no thought for the meticulous gardener, scattering volcanic spoils of soil over the turf. Their showy attire means they can also be singled out on blossoming fruit trees and their favourite common garden flowers, such as dandelions and alkanet.

In Australia, there is an eye-catching solitary bee that goes by the name of the teddy bear bee (*Amegilla bombiformis*), because her cute bumblebee shape and bright orangey-brown coat make her look like a cuddly toy.

The majority of solitary bees are less instantly recognizable. Often, only a slight distinguishing feature, such as a hairstyle or a body marking, provides the clue. Take the thousands of buff-and-black-striped mining bee species. Red-girdled, long-fringed and big-headed are some of the more entertaining names they have been given to tell them apart.

Likewise, thousands of tiny bees known collectively as furrow bees or as sweat bees (because in hot countries they can obtain valuable moisture and salts by sucking perspiration from humans and animals), have been given names such as orange-legged, white-footed, red-backed, broad-faced and sharp-collared. These underground nesters are found all over the world, but are generally too small – averaging only 5–10mm (0.2–0.4in) in length – to be readily observed.

Many sweat bees, with their metallic blue or green sheen, look more like small flies than bees. Among them, the common furrow bee (*Lasioglossum calceatum*) and the green furrow bee (*Lasioglossum morio*), glisten in the

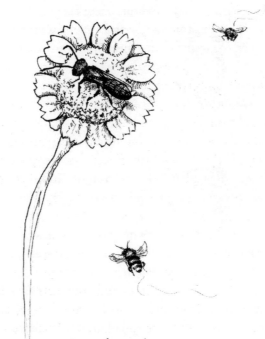

Green furrow bee

sunlight like jewels. Others, like the bull-headed furrow bee (*Lasioglossum zonulum*), are black with smooth, shiny elongated bodies.

We didn't realize that the tiny black flying insects we saw in a garden last summer were bees until we walked over and found a block of wood with holes drilled in it. They had partitioned the hollow cavity into individual cells using tree resin, then laid their eggs and provisioned pollen. Now they were plugging the entrance of the nest with bits of stone and sand. They used their full body weight to push the tiny fragments into position, creating a mosaic that eventually formed a front door. It was fascinating to watch these bees persevere, and a little sad knowing that once this job was complete, their short lives would soon be over.

When it comes to choosing a nesting location, the availability of homemaking materials is just as important to bees as a plentiful food supply. There were so many resin bees in the garden we visited because it was being landscaped utilizing the materials the bees like using to construct their nest. This also explains why the wool carder bee is a frequent visitor to our garden when the lamb's ear (*Stachys byzantina*) is out. She is collecting the soft downy material from the underside of the leaves. It is fascinating to watch her industriousness; teasing out the fibres, rolling them into a ball nearly as big as herself, and flying home to partition and plug her nest. In central and

Wool carder bee on lamb's ear

southern Europe, *Anthidium florentinum*, one of several European wool carders, teases out the fluffy down from the seed heads of dandelions for her nest.

By the end of summer, most of our bee visitors have died, and others are waning. But in early autumn the ivy mining bee emerges to feed on ivy pollen and nectar. Her short lifespan is perfectly synchronized with the flowering of the ivy, which provides all the sustenance she needs.

⋆ Fussy eaters ⋆

Like the ivy mining bee, many other solitary bees have evolved to live off the pollen of one family of flowers. This specialism is called oligolecty. Many of these bees derive their common name from those flowers, such as the clover bee (*Melitta leporina*) and the heather bee (*Colletes succinctus*).

The most famous oligolectic bees are the 200 species of brightly coloured orchid bees in Central and South America. The orchid flower, whose 'prurient apparitions' so offended Victorian critic John Ruskin, has devised an unorthodox method of sex. It lures the male orchid bee by emitting a scent that resembles the female bee. The duped male attempts to copulate with the flower, and in the act gets pollen stuck to his back. When the hoodwinked bee later falls for the same trick by another orchid, he transfers the pollen to it. Some orchid species use this ruse to avoid having to produce nectar for their pollinators, but other orchids do offer a prize – a chemical whose perfume the male bee has to collect if he is to have any hope of attracting a female.

✦ Gatecrashers ✦

A quarter of solitary bee species have no housebuilding skills. They are cleptoparasites, or cuckoo bees, which take over the nests of other species. There are at least 5,000 species of solitary cuckoo bees. Many, such as the blood bees (so-called because of their red abdomens) and the sharp-tailed bees, which look more like zebra-striped wasps, only occupy the home of one host species. Others, such as some nomad bees, are opportunist burglars, breaking into the home of many different species.

The hairy-footed flower bee has a cleptoparasite in the common mourning bee (*Melecta albifrons*), who has striking white spots down the side of her dark, fluffy abdomen. But don't be fooled by her cute appearance;

she shows no mercy to our flower bee. She will sneak into the nest and lay her own eggs, which will hatch first and gobble up the flower bees' eggs or larvae and all the stored pollen. Sharp-tailed bees are cuckoos of leafcutter bees, and their presence is usually a good indicator that leafcutter bees are nesting nearby.

There is no point in trying to intervene to defend these cuckooed bees. Nature works in mysterious ways, and we must respect that. If you see cuckoo bees it means the population of its host is healthy.

New bee on the block

New solitary bees are being identified all the time. One was found in the US in 2009 after having been confused for years with some of the other 200 bee species living in the same city. The tiny sweat bee, just a few millimetres long, is aptly called the Gotham bee (*Lasioglossum gotham*) on account of its discovery in New York's Botanical Garden.

✦ Signs of social behaviour ✦

In the hugely diverse world of solitary bees, not all are hermits. Some species exhibit a primitive form of social behaviour, living as a family and dividing labour. Among them are the carpenter bees, where mum sticks around to raise her daughters and they share foraging and guarding duties between them.

Many of the 4,000 tiny sweat and furrow bees are even more social. In one season, the matriarch bee can produce two or three generations of sterile daughters, who live a communal existence, carrying out chores under her watchful gaze. By late summer, she produces males and fertile females who will mate with bees from neighbouring nests and continue this semi-social existence in their new family.

This primitive eusociality is thought to have evolved around 20 million years ago.

There is no doubt that the importance of solitary bees has hitherto been sorely overlooked. Hopefully that will change, as new techniques such as DNA sequencing and digital imaging allow scientists to identify new species and give them popular names. The ivy mining bee was only recognized as a distinct species and given a scientific name in 1993. It has since been recorded across Europe and more recently was added to the tally of 250 bees across the British Isles, along with the viper's bugloss mason bee (*Hoplitis adunca*), first seen in Britain in 2016 – nesting in a bee hotel in a London park.

Blue bees

Nature doesn't give us many blue birds, mammals or insects. So the flash of a kingfisher, or a peacock's plumage is a rare delight. The blue carpenter bee (*Xylocopa caerulea*) is one dazzling example. Common in southern China, India and South East Asia, this large bee (up to 23mm/0.9in in length), is covered from thorax to partway down her abdomen in bright blue hairs giving the impression of wearing a fluffy blue jacket over her black body.

Some small sweat bees glisten an iridescent blue or green, but cannot compete with the striking appearance of the big blue bee.

CHAPTER 2

Bees and Us

Humankind's relationship with bees goes back to the birth of Homo sapiens. Cave dwellers hunted bees for their honey and in southern Africa there are dozens of rock paintings of honey hunting, dating from 20,000 years ago. But probably the most famous depiction of this dangerous pastime is a wall painting in northern Spain that shows two human figures on a rope ladder, ascending a cliff face. One has an arm thrust into the bees' nest as the bees hover around, while the other holds what looks like a basket to

collect the bounty. This Bicorp painting in the Spider Cave near present-day Santander is around 10,000 years old. It demonstrates just how highly valued honey was as an energy food, a natural sweetener and for making one of the first fermented alcoholic beverages.

◆ Beekeeping ◆

The practice of honey hunting is still carried out in some parts of Asia where the wild, giant honeybee species nest on the edges of high clifftops. But smaller western and eastern honeybees have been managed since the ancient Egyptians and Chinese took up beekeeping some 3,000 years ago.

When we collected our first colony of honeybees in a small travelling box we were dimly aware that we were following a tradition that stretched back to antiquity. Then bees were kept in clay hives shaped like giant thimbles, which are depicted in stone bas-reliefs in Egyptian temples. The ancient Roman poet Virgil wrote one of the first practical beekeepers' theses in book IV of the *Georgics*, published around 30 BC, in which he vividly described the workings of the beehive, from the 'the work-shy gang' of drones to the foragers 'employed in getting food, and by fixed agreement, work on the fields'. It provided farmers with advice still useful today. To 'find your bees a settled sure abode, where neither winds can enter' and neither sheep nor goats 'tread down the flowers'.

Monasteries and abbeys that were at the heart of European medieval society produced their own honey, the alcoholic honey drink mead, and beeswax for candles. On land next to their orchards, they set aside areas for

Bee deities

In ancient Greek mythology, Aristaeus was the god of beekeeping. The Mayans, who kept stingless bees in wooden logs in their temples in the forests of Central America, also had a patron deity of beekeepers, Mok Chi. Twice a year, their priests gave offerings to the gods in a ceremony, asking permission to harvest the honey. There are even Christian saints of beekeeping: the fourth-century Bishop of Milan, St Ambrose, and St Gobnait, an Irish nun who lived in the sixth century (see page 128).

beehives called apiaries, and practiced apiculture, the art of keeping honeybees.

Mayan priests practiced meliponiculture, keeping stingless honey-making bees, known as *xunan-kab* (royal lady), who they regarded as a gift from the gods. Mayan hieroglyphic texts include passages about beekeeping.

✦ Honey ✦

Honey was vitally important, not just as a sweetener, but also as a symbol of sweetness and love, so that the industrious bees that made it were venerated in many ancient religions and early civilizations. Honey was considered ambrosia, the food of gods. It has been found, still edible, buried in ancient Egyptian pyramids, alongside the mummified remains of pharaohs, intended to sweeten the afterlife.

The Hindu god of love, Kama, carries a bow with a string made of bees. His Greek and Roman counterparts, Eros and Cupid, dipped their arrows in honey.

The bee was often seen as a celestial creature that filled the gap between human beings and the divine. Virgil starts his beekeeping thesis with 'Of air-born honey, gift of heaven'. And Roman encyclopaedist Pliny the Elder described nectar as the 'sweat of heavens' and the 'saliva of the stars'.

Honey was turned into one of the earliest fermented alcoholic drinks, called *balché* by the Mayans, but we know it better as mead. It was central to wedding celebrations in Greco-Roman culture and throughout medieval Europe, with newlyweds drinking mead for a month after their marriage to bring luck, happiness and to conceive a son. The ritual is one possible source of the word honeymoon. Today, honey wine, known as tej, is still the national drink of Ethiopia, where it's been brewed for 5,000 years.

✦ Medicine ✦

Honey has long been revered as a medicine because of its antiviral, anti-inflammatory, antibacterial and antiseptic properties. It's been used in traditional remedies for thousands of years to treat an A-Z of ailments from arthritis to hay fever, sore throats to ulcers. Ancient Chinese, Indian Ayruverdic and Mayan medicine, still practiced today, include many prescriptions containing honey.

Hippocrates, the father of modern medicine, frequently promoted honey to his patients. Aristotle thought it good for leading a long life and for digestion. And in the Islamic religion, the Qur'an has a chapter, called 'The Bees', in which honey is described as coming from the bees' bellies:

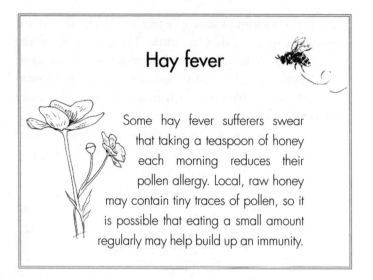

Hay fever

Some hay fever sufferers swear that taking a teaspoon of honey each morning reduces their pollen allergy. Local, raw honey may contain tiny traces of pollen, so it is possible that eating a small amount regularly may help build up an immunity.

'a drink of varying colour wherein is healing for men'.

Honey was used for dressing wounds and even today some medically licensed wound-care dressings contain honey. Its high sugar and low water content, low acidity, and small amounts of hydrogen peroxide, which releases oxygen on contact with the skin, account for its antimicrobial qualities. It may help to prevent scarring by drawing in moisture and promoting the growth of new skin. Tests also indicate that combining honey with certain antibiotics can make them more successful at fighting drug-resistant superbugs such as MRSA.

In recent years, manuka honey has been touted for its superior medicinal properties. The nectar from the manuka bush (also known as the tea tree) has high levels of a compound called dihydroxyacetone. This chemical produces methylglyoxal, which may give manuka honey slightly higher antibacterial and cell-killing properties.

Nutritionally, all honey contains about 80 per cent sugar in a simple predigested form that can be directly absorbed by the human body. This is why it can aid digestion, as Aristotle observed. The remainder is a mixture of water, minerals – which may include traces of phosphorus, calcium, magnesium, iron, zinc, potassium, selenium and manganese – and tiny amounts of vitamin B and vitamin C.

Honey lost its monopoly as a sweetener in Europe in the eighteenth and nineteenth centuries with the arrival of cheap, imported sugar cane and sugar beet, but it is now valued as a healthier alternative to refined sugar and artificial sweeteners.

✦ Harvesting ✦

The first time we harvested our honey was a magical and emotional experience. We felt that we had nurtured our bees through a long, hot summer and hoped that, in return

Honey drink cold remedy

Honey has been used throughout the ages to treat sore throats and colds. Even today, a soothing hot drink made of honey and lemon just before bedtime can aid recovery.

2 tablespoons lemon juice
(about half a lemon's worth)
1 tablespoon of clear runny honey
A mugful of hot water (not boiling)
Cinnamon stick (optional)

Mix the lemon juice and honey in a mug. Add hot water, poured from a kettle just before it boils, to fill the mug.

Stir well and add a cinnamon stick. If it's too sharp, add a little more honey until the taste is more palatable.

for our careful husbandry, they were happy to share some of the spoils of their labour. The second year, they came through a cold spring and a rainy summer, so there was less honey to go round. But when you appreciate the effort the bees put into making just a fraction of a teaspoon of the golden liquid (see page 54), you are grateful for receiving any.

As a beekeeper, you soon realize that there is no average colony, or average year. A high honey yield depends on there being good weather so the bees can forage when the trees and flowers are in bloom, an abundance of these nectar sources, and a strong and healthy colony of bees.

The shelves in our living room are piled high with jars of honey from each of our harvests, labelled with the date and location of the apiary. A few of the honeys are still as clear and runny as the day they came out of the hive, others are solid. Some are a rich amber colour but most are paler. They are a visual reminder of the varieties of honey the bees produce according to the available nectar. One year the honey tasted of elderflower, but mostly it has a slight hint of citrus or mint that we have come to recognize as the lime trees – also known as linden, tilia or basswood – that line the parks and streets of many cities in the northern hemisphere, and are smothered in tiny white flowers just past midsummer.

Honeybees generally fly within a 5km (3 mile) radius of their hive in search of nectar. In towns and cities with

Honey miles

Astonishingly, a colony of honeybees is thought to fly around 55,000 miles – the equivalent of one and a half times around the world – to make just 1kg (2.2lbs) of honey (see Busy busy bees, page 55). An average hive, in an average year, can produce about 18kgs (40lbs) of honey, which means the bees will have covered a combined total of 2 million miles.

flower-filled gardens, parks full of trees, railway sidings and derelict land, where buddleia and other wild plants and shrubs freely seed themselves, bees may travel less than a mile. Their honey will be polyfloral, containing nectar from a huge variety of flowers, even if one source is dominant. In contrast, monofloral honey comes from hives placed in fields or orchards of one flowering crop for as far as the eye can see.

There are some 300 different types of recognized honey, and on a trip to any supermarket you can find a bewildering array of varieties from all corners of the planet. Each has a distinctive colour and flavour depending on which flowers the bees have been foraging: from highly perfumed French lavender to spicy Tasmanian leatherwood, herbal Greek thyme and toffee-like heather from the remote Scottish Highlands.

Colours range from almost transparent to near black. In general, the lighter the honey, the milder the taste. Darker honey can have a strong, pungent and even slightly bitter flavour, but is thought to be higher in minerals and antioxidants. Some of our favourites include buckwheat honey from the plains of North America, which has a deep, malty taste, and chestnut honey, from the sweet chestnut forests of France and Spain, with its delicious, earthy flavour and treacle-like consistency.

Viscosity varies hugely. Acacia honey is popular worldwide for its delicate taste and runny consistency;

heather honey has a jelly-like texture; while some crystallize quickly – in particular, rapeseed honey, which has to be harvested early because it can harden on the honeycomb.

Crystallization, also referred to as granulation, is a natural process by which honey turns from a liquid to semi-solid state. It can be reversed by gentle heating.

Much commercially produced honey has been heat-treated to delay crystallization. This is similar to pasteurization for milk. The honey will also have been processed by filtration to remove pollen grains. Cheaper honey tends to be blended to create a consistent taste combination that can be replicated. If you read the small print on the label, it will often say that the jar contains a blend of honeys from the EU, or rest of the world. China, New Zealand (the home of manuka honey) and Argentina are the world's top honey exporters by value.

Whipped, churned or creamed honey are other processes that make the honey a smooth, spreadable consistency. But all industrial processes remove some of the goodness from the honey.

✦ Raw honey ✦

Raw honey has been extracted from the hive with none of the goodness taken out. It is simply spun off the comb, strained through a large sieve without removing the tiny pollen grains, left to settle in a large honey bucket for twenty-four hours, and then poured into sterilized jars. Chunks of raw, chewy honeycomb can be cut straight off the comb. Most hobby beekeepers with a few hives use this method to harvest the honey.

✦ Organic honey ✦

For honey to be certified organic, the beekeeper needs to be able to establish that, within a certain radius around their apiary (this varies according to which country's rules you are following), nectar and pollen sources have not come into contact with weedkillers, pesticides, other chemicals, or genetically modified crops. In the UK, perhaps only heather honey could meet these strict criteria. The world's first organic honey was certified in 1983. It came from wild bees deep in the tropical rainforests of Zambia.

Blackberry and mint mocktail

This fruity summer drink is suitable for parties and picnics. It's very easy and quick to make and is delicious, healthy and not too sweet. This recipe is for two glasses – simply multiply the quantities for more guests.

1 large handful of fresh (or defrosted) blackberries*
1 handful of fresh mint leaves*
¼ cup of honey
Juice of 1 lemon
½ a cup of water
2 cups of sparkling water

*Save a few to garnish the drink

Put the blackberries, mint and
honey into a cocktail shaker
and crush with a muddle.
If you don't have a shaker
or a muddle, you could use
a pestle and mortar and
then tip the crushed
ingredients into a large jar.

Add the lemon juice and
1 cup of water, cover and
shake well to mix.

Strain the liquid into two glasses
with ice, then top each glass
with the remaining sparkling water.

Garnish with a few blackberries
and mint leaves.

✦ Stingless bee honey ✦

Stingless bees in the Yucatan peninsular of Mexico make organic honey. It is a lighter colour and has a higher water content – from 25–35 per cent – than honey made by honeybees. Stingless bees tend to live in smaller colonies than honeybees, and make much smaller quantities of honey, nearer 3kg (7lbs) than 18kg (40lbs).

Honey from Australia's *Tetragonula* stingless bees by all accounts has a sharp citrus, or eucalyptus tang that comes from the resin and wax pots in which they store their honey. Another species of its native sugarbag bee, the *Austroplebeia*, stores its honey in pots made only from wax, giving the honey a much milder flavour. Taking honey from the stingless bees' small wax pots often means destroying the colony, as it cannot be kept in moveable frame hives.

✦ Pollution and honey ✦

Little research has been done into pollution and honey. A small study in Vancouver, Canada, that used geochemical and isotopic analysis, like fingerprinting, to detect minuscule levels of lead, zinc, arsenic, copper and cadmium, found the city's honey to be totally safe to eat. Air pollutants, such as diesel exhaust fumes, are unlikely to come into contact with honey since most flowers only secrete nectar for a short period each day from nectaries deep inside the flower, it is sucked up by the bee's straw-like tongue and then placed into beeswax cells, which have anti-pathogenic properties.

In a 2017 worldwide study, traces of pesticides were detected in honey samples collected from all continents, but at such miniscule levels that they fell far below the maximum permitted in food for humans.

Blue honey!

Bees don't always forage on nectar if there is an alternative source of sugar nearby. A French apiary discovered this when its bees produced an unusual blue-coloured 'honey'. It turned out that the bees had been foraging on the waste products of a local M&M sweets factory.

✦ Beeswax ✦

Beeswax created artificial light for centuries, until the mass production of cheaper paraffin wax. Beeswax candles lit up church altars, religious ceremonies and great halls, where their clean smoke and sweet smell were highly valued, in comparison to the greasy, black smoke produced by tallow candles, made from animal fat. Beekeeping boomed in Europe during the Great Plague (1347–1350) because beeswax candles were used in funeral ceremonies. Wherever the Catholic Church spread, so too did the making of beeswax candles, and it was not until 1900 that a papal decree permitted Catholic churches to use non-100-per-cent-beeswax candles. Although humans no longer rely on beeswax to see in the dark, we still appreciate the sweet fragrance and warm glow of its candles.

Beeswax starts as a tiny flake (like a fish scale), and when the bees collect and manipulate thousands of these flakes they form solid building blocks. It is a tactile substance, malleable at ambient temperatures. How many of us have played with warm candle wax? We seem to be fascinated by the way it melts and then solidifies again and can be moulded and shaped.

Beeswax is also waterproof and has antipathogenic properties, all of which have made it a hugely versatile and

Wax works

● Worker bees aged between twelve and eighteen days secrete wax scales the size of a pinhead from glands underneath their abdomens.

● It takes about 500,000 scales to make 450g (1lb) of beeswax.

● To extract 450g (1lb) of beeswax from the wax cappings, or the 'lids' of honeycomb, requires harvesting about 4kg (8.5lbs) of honey. The cappings are collected with a special uncapping fork, then washed and rendered in hot water. When the wax is liquid it is strained through a fine cloth mesh to remove the debris, leaving a block of wax when it cools. This process may have to be repeated until a clean block is produced.

valuable commodity. Ancient Egyptians embalmed bodies, sealed coffins and mummified pharaohs with it. It was also used to preserve writings on parchment, seal legal documents, and as an early glue. The Mayans used a wax resin substance, called cerumen, made by stingless bees to fix feathers to their arrows. In Greek mythology, when Icarus dared to fly too near the sun with wings made of feathers and beeswax, the adhesive melted and he fell to his death.

We have stacks of beautiful yellow beeswax blocks piled high in our shed. At a distance they look like rounds of cheese. When the wax is freshly made by the bees for honeycomb it's a bright white colour, but turns yellow when the wax becomes stained with propolis (tree resin) and pollen. We love the colour and the aroma, a combination of sweet honey, the spicy fragrance of the propolis, and cedar wood from the hive.

We give away some of our beeswax to people who want to make home-made cosmetic creams, candles, soap, natural furniture polish, dubbing for leather, alternative food wrap to plastic, to rub into the wood of musical instruments, and to artists for paintings, sculpture or casting jewellery – all activities that have been practiced for thousands of years. In Australia, wax mixed with resin rock paintings depicting animals and humans have been dated as 4,000 years old. The mouthpieces of Aboriginals' didgeridoos were made of wax and resin from their stingless bees.

Ancient cultures also recognized beeswax for its health benefits, such as treating wounds, its beauty enhancements and anti-aging properties. Today, much of the world's beeswax comes from China, India and Ethiopia (where it's a by-product of brewing tej) and it is used in the global manufacture of cosmetics. It's a natural emulsifier that helps lotions to bind, creates a sheen in lipsticks and is a lubricant for moustache and beard styling. In addition, the pharmaceutical industry uses beeswax in ointments and for coating pills and suppositories.

◦ Apitherapy ◦

Imagine a beehive as a human medicine cabinet and beauty parlour. Within it are many other natural products that can enhance our health and well-being. Apitherapy is the practice of using all the products in the hive for healing.

Propolis is a dark, sticky, tree resin that bees collect to maintain a germ-free hive. Its antiseptic, antibacterial, and antifungal qualities have long been used to treat toothache and gum problems, and it's an ingredient today in natural toothpastes and eczema creams.

Pollen grains are rich in proteins, amino acids and vitamins, including the B-complex and folic acid and can be eaten, sprinkled over food.

Royal jelly is a creamy excretion from the hypopharyngeal and mandibular glands in the worker bees' bodies to feed developing larvae. Those larvae fed copious amounts of this protein-rich food develop into queen bees. It is hailed as the elixir of youth and added to creams touted for their youth-enhancing powers. One of its most famous proponents is the fictional detective Sherlock Holmes, who discovered its potency in his laboratory at his home on the Sussex Downs where he had retired and taken up beekeeping. Today, the commercial production of royal jelly is on an industrial scale, involving a number of methods, including grafting millions of worker bee larvae into artificial plastic queen cells.

While human health and well-being is important, let's not forget that the honeybee colony requires all these hive products for its own survival. The bees' needs should always take priority over human vanity and greed.

✦ Hives ✦

Until the 1850s, western honeybees were kept in baskets: a conical willow or hazel basket, called an alveary, waterproofed with a layer of cow manure mixed with ashes or lime; or a straw basket called a skep. The baskets were often tucked into purpose-made alcoves in walls, to shelter them from the rain. These bee boules can still be seen in seventeenth- and eighteenth-century country houses in Britain and Ireland. The main problem with skep beekeeping was that the colony had to be killed at the end of the summer to retrieve the honey.

The practice was transformed in the mid-nineteenth century by the invention of the moveable frame hive – a wooden box containing a number of frames on which the bees build their vertical sheets of wax honeycomb. The frames are lifted out of the box without destroying the colony. It was patented in the US by the Reverend L. L. Langstroth, whose first box was reputedly an empty champagne crate. His eponymous hive is still popular in the USA and variations of it are used all over the world, from the standard British National Hive and French Dadant (named after Charles Dadant, a French-American apiarist). The boxes come in two depths: the deeper one is known as the brood box as it holds the queen and her brood (developing larvae); while the shallow boxes, known as supers (Latin

Skep

Langstroth

Top bar

William Broughton Carr

Different styles of honeybee hives

for 'on top') are placed above the brood box for the bees to store their honey. A number of these honey boxes can be added to allow the bees to make and store more and more honey over the summer. It is the reason the hive grows in height.

The image many people have of a hive is one with sloping sides, a gabled roof and white-painted timber weatherboarding, set in a pretty cottage garden. British amateur apiarist, William Broughton Carr, was responsible for this attractive design at the turn of the twentieth century.

The moveable frames are usually constructed with foundation, a pre-made uniform rectangular sheet of beeswax moulded on both sides with impressions of the honeycomb hexagons. The bees 'draw out' the flat foundation by adding their own wax to the hexagonal impressions to make the walls of their cells. A sheet of foundation for a British National hive brood box has 7,500 cells.

A top-bar hive allows bees to build their own vertical honeycomb. This hive is more popular in many parts of Africa because it can be easily built using cheap local materials. On other continents, some hobby beekeepers have adopted this style of beekeeping, although the beautifully curved sheets of wax can be difficult to manage and to remove intact.

In 2015, two Australians invented a new type of hive with a tap, out of which flows honey, like beer from a barrel. We, like everyone else, were initially intrigued by the flow hive. The idea is that the bees build their own wax onto a plastic foundation to make cells that they fill with nectar and cap with wax. When the honey tap is turned, the cells crack and the hexagons turn into channels allowing the honey to flow down into a trough and into a jar held under the tap. Once the comb is drained the tap is reset and the hexagonal comb reverts to its original shape.

Throughout history inventive beekeepers have tried to make beekeeping easier, but it takes patience, attention to the natural world and an understanding of how the colony works in nature to master the art and skill of beekeeping. There are no short cuts.

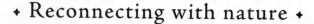

⋆ Reconnecting with nature ⋆

When we brought our first bees home, we were unconsciously looking for a way to reconnect with nature. Inside the travelling box were 10,000 worker bees and one queen, which we were going to rehouse into their permanent home – a British National Hive made of cedar wood.

Mustard and honey salad dressing

This delicious salad dressing is easy and quick to make. The hot mustard combines with the sweetness of the honey and the sharpness of the vinegar to create a rich dressing that goes with most salads and can also be used as a marinade for chicken or drizzled on roasted vegetables.

1 tablespoon clear runny honey
1 tablespoon Dijon mustard (wholegrain also works well)
1 tablespoon balsamic vinegar
1 clove of garlic, crushed
Pinch of salt and freshly ground black pepper
4 tablespoons olive oil

Mix together the first five ingredients in a lidded jar.

Add the oil and shake together.

This dressing will keep well in a jar in the larder. Shake well just before using.

We tipped the small colony of bees, called a nucleus, into our hive and, with a gentle smack on the bottom of the box, the majority of the bees fell into their new larger home. With the lid on the new home, we placed the box next to the small entrance at the bottom of the hive.

It was fascinating to watch the stragglers slowly find their way to the entrance and disappear into the darkness of the hive.

By closely observing the bees, we began to see that some were standing stationary and fanning their wings while others were walking around the external woodwork and others flying in increasingly larger circles above our heads. What we were watching was a new animal orientate and get used to its new home by means of touch, smell and sight.

The stationary bees standing near the entrance were gripping the structure tightly with their clawed toes, while fanning their wings. This fanning sent out wafts of air laden with a scent from the Nasonov gland at the back of their abdomens. It directs the other bees to the entrance. It's a message that says 'home this way'.

Other bees were using glands on their feet that lay down a scent trail to deter bees from another colony from entering. Colonies of honeybees don't usually mix. Each colony will defend itself against intruders.

That first day, watching the bees through our veils was an education into a new world. A world of trees, plants,

Biophilia

The Pulitzer Prize-winning biologist E. O. Wilson believes that humans have an innate and genetically determined affinity with the natural world, a concept he calls biophilia. But working day in, day out in the artificial environment of an office, or factory, stifles our biophilia by cutting us off from the changing seasons and other natural phenomena, and, as a result, our psychological and emotional development suffers. Richard Louv, the author of *Last Child in the Woods* (2010), coined the term 'nature-deficit disorder' to describe such a condition in children who have had little contact with nature.

insects and the history and future of the natural world no less.

But we didn't know that at the time.

Reconnecting with nature is one of the reasons behind a recent explosion in hobby beekeeping in urban areas. Another is that with threats to bees from the use of pesticides in the countryside and loss of wild flower meadows (see page 144), bees often fare better in towns and cities where gardens, parks, green rooftops and tree-lined streets provide a diverse year-round diet.

Whatever one's motivations for beekeeping, the key to doing it well is in understanding how the animal, the colony of honeybees, operates. This book is not a guide to beekeeping. There are plenty to choose from, but our advice to getting started is to join a local beekeeping association, take a beginners' course, and shadow an experienced beekeeper for a season, before getting your own beehive. You may discover that it takes more time that you can spare at this stage in your life, or that the location you had in mind isn't suitable for a hive, or even that you are severely allergic to bee stings. If that's the case, don't worry, there are many better ways to help bees than by keeping honeybees (see Chapter 4). The wild solitary bees and bumblebees' homes are being destroyed by relentless urban expansion and development. They need our help even more than the hive dwellers (see page 168).

Urban bumblebees

⋆ The elephants and the bees ⋆

In Celtic folklore, the sixth-century Irish patron saint of bees and beekeeping, St Gobnait, is famous for driving cattle thieves from convent land by hurling skeps (woven basket beehives) of bees at them. In 2008, a charity, Save the Elephants, adapted her methods to deter crop raiders in Kenya. Here, however, the thieves were herds of elephants, and conflict between the animals and villagers had led to many elephants being shot. The charity's Lucy King came up with the ingenious idea of using beekeeping to both prevent the death of more elephants and protect villagers' crops. Elephants are scared of honeybees. If threatened, honeybees will sting an elephant's only weak spot – its eyes. So, Save the Elephants erected fences made of wire attached to beehives around four community growing areas in Kenya to keep out the elephants. If the wire is tripped by the elephants, angry bees emerge and the alarmed elephants scarper, never to return. Not only has the beehive fence been a resounding success, but the bees also pollinate crops and increase yields, as well as producing honey that villagers can sell for extra income. And the elephants are no longer shot. The award-winning Elephants and Bees project has now spread to many villages on the front line of elephant crop raiding in different parts of Africa, as well as India and Nepal.

Elephant bee fence

✦ The beehive metaphor ✦

The social behaviour and industriousness of the honeybee colony has fascinated humans, nearly as much as its produce. No other creature has been used as a metaphor for how societies and economies should, or could be, run, or as a commentary on the politics of the day, from feudal hierarchies to unbridled capitalism, socialist utopias and totalitarian dystopias.

Until 1586, the ruler of the beehive was assumed to be a king. After she was correctly identified as a queen bee who laid eggs, Charles Butler wrote *The Feminine Monarchie, or the History of Bees*, published in 1609 to celebrate the reign of Elizabeth I.

A century later, Bernard de Mandeville's *Fable of the Bees* (1714) is an early blueprint for laissez-faire capitalism. In France, Enlightenment thinkers tried to show that the hive made the case against absolute monarchy: Jean-Baptiste Simon, for example, called his revolutionary book, *The Republic of Bees* (1740). The eighteenth-century French republic adopted the hexagonal shape of the honeycomb as its symbol. But the bee was soon appropriated for the service of dictatorship when Napoleon crowned himself emperor wearing a robe embroidered with imperial gold bees.

In America, the immigrant European honeybee became synonymous with the country's fight for independence. According to an essay on bees by the US naturalist John Burroughs, in 1879, the honeybee epitomized the settlers' spirit. 'She has the white man's craftiness, his industry, his architectural skills, his neatness and love of system, his foresight; and above all his eager, miserly habits. The honeybee's great ambition is to lay up great stores.' The beehive is still the emblem of the Mormon state of Utah.

The first national trade union-sponsored newspaper published in 1862 was called the *Bee-Hive*, which became the official paper of the International Working Men's Association. For many in Victorian England, however, the beehive was not simply the proud symbol of hard work, but also the acceptance of the social order, nowhere more so than in Manchester's neo-Gothic town hall, where floor mosaics depicting bees celebrate the city's position at the centre of Britain's Industrial Revolution. Today, the bee has come to symbolize Manchester's heritage, but also its indomitable spirit following a terrorist bombing in 2017.

The hexagonal wax comb perfectly crafted by the bees inspired other fields of human endeavour, such as modernist architecture and design. Many architects –

including the Spanish Antonio Gaudi; Mies van der Rohe, pioneer of the Bauhaus movement; the American Frank Lloyd Wright; and the French-Swiss Le Corbusier – are said to have been influenced by honeycomb.

But it is not just from the hive that humankind can learn. The pollination services of wild bees provide lessons about the importance of living in harmony with nature.

As Buddhist texts note, bees take what they need to survive without harming the beauty and vitality of their source of sustenance. For humans, to act in the manner of bees would result in compassionate and conscious living.

+ Pollination +

Approximately one in three mouthfuls that the average person eats has been pollinated by bees, including most fruits, vegetables, seeds, nuts, herbs, spices and oil crops. Together they supply a major proportion of nutrients in the human diet. In addition, bees pollinate coffee, and fodder crops for meat and dairy cattle, and other livestock. And it's not just the food on our plate that we need to thank nature's master pollinator for: plant-derived medicines such as aspirin and morphine; fibres such as cotton and linen; and trees that supply timber for construction and are the lungs of the planet, are all pollinated by bees. A few crops are totally reliant on bee pollination to form fruits or seeds, but for the most part bee pollination boosts yields by as much as 75 per cent, increases the size and improves the shape, sweetness and shelf life of ninety commercially produced crops.

The annual contribution of pollinators to the global economy has recently been estimated at up to $577bn. Among insect pollinators, bees are recognized as the largest and most important. While managed honeybees are now responsible for a staggering 80 per cent of insect pollination, the 25,000 or so wild bee species have been pollinating native crops and vegetation for millennia.

In the Americas and Antipodes there were no honeybees until they arrived with the European colonizers. The 'white man's fly', as Native Americans called them, were brought on ships with seeds and samplings to create orchards and clover pastures. The poet Emily Dickinson later wrote: 'To make a prairie it takes a clover and one honeybee.'

Yet there were already wild, solitary bees on both continents. While the indigenous people recognized these bees' valuable contribution to pollination, their services went largely unnoticed by everyone else until relatively recently.

In Utah, for example, farmers didn't realize that a native bee had been pollinating their alfalfa crop until the 1940s, when they started ploughing over their land and using pesticides to expand cultivation, only to see a dramatic drop in yields because they had destroyed the wild alkali bees' *(Nomia melanderi)* habitat and poisoned its forage.

Modern farming worldwide has become increasingly reliant on trucking in managed honeybees to do the job of pollination because it has wiped out wild bees' habitat, depriving them of food and shelter. Nowhere is this more visible than in Central Valley, California, where 82 per cent of the world's almonds are grown. More than 1 million acres are now planted with almond trees that stretch for more than 400 miles. They blossom in the middle of February and require billions of bees to pollinate them. Three weeks later, the region reverts to a desert unable to sustain any wild pollinators. So each year 2 million honeybee hives have to be trucked in from all over the US in the biggest migratory pollination event on the planet.

Just as agriculture has become industrialized, so too has the pollination process. The hives, almost 500 of them, stacked four high, strapped onto some 4,000 trucks, come from as far as Florida. And after twenty-two days pollinating the almonds, the hives are back on the trucks heading for Washington State to pollinate apples, then to the north-east for cranberries, pumpkins and blueberries, even though honeybees are far less efficient pollinators of these crops than native wild bees.

The native North American blue orchard mason bee is prized for its efficiency at pollinating a wide variety of fruit trees. In Europe, the native orchard mason bee

(*Osmia cornuta*), and common red mason bee are similarly efficient pollinators of oilseed rape, soft fruits, and fruit trees. In Japan, which has 390 native bee species, its horn-faced mason bee (*Osmia cornifrons*) has been found to be eighty times more effective than honeybees at pollinating apples and is now responsible for up to 70 per cent of the country's crop.

Mason bees are more efficient pollinators because they land directly on the reproductive structure of the fruit tree blossom and the bees' scopa gets loaded with pollen, which they deposit onto the stigma of the next blossom they visit.

The Japanese native shaggy fuzzyfoot flower bee (*Anthophora pilipes*) is so superior a buzz pollinator of blueberries that it has been imported into the US to help do the job. The North American squash bee (*Peponapis pruinosa*) is a highly effective pollinator of squashes, pumpkins and zucchini because it is able to withstand the cold, and flies very early in the morning before daylight. The bee has adapted to fly at this time, before other bees, to plunder the nectar and pollen, which the massive tubular flower heads release when they open up in the dark.

Another early flier, the North American sunflower leafcutter bee, which also goes by the splendid name of the pugnacious leafcutter (*Megachile pugnata*), is a skilled pollinator of the large-headed yellow flowers grown on a vast scale for their seeds and oil.

Squash bees

Some native wild pollinators are now managed to aid crop pollination. Farmers create areas of habitat for bees who nest underground, and 'bee hotels' (see page 169) are strategically placed in orchards for cavity-nesting mason bees to check into, and fields of alfalfa for alfalfa leafcutter bees to nest in. These European bees tripled seed production when they were first imported to the US in the 1930s and are now thought to be responsible for two thirds of the crop's production worldwide. An alfafa leafcutter can visit and pollinate more than a thousand alfalfa flowers a day because, unlike other bees, it doesn't mind receiving what has been termed as a floral slap-in-the-face by the flower's lower petal, the keel. When the bee puts pressure on the petal to snap open to reveal the nectar and pollen, the keel hits the visitor.

Yet despite being better pollinators of many crops than honeybees, solitary bees are not deemed commercially viable in most cases because they reproduce much more slowly and in much smaller numbers, so they are often viewed simply as an insurance policy in case of problems with the apian workforce.

The paid-for pollinator workforce also includes commercially bred buff-tailed bumblebees. They are exported around the world in their millions each year from factories in the Netherlands and Belgium to buzz pollinate tomatoes, aubergines (eggplant), courgettes (zucchini), chillies and (bell) peppers in polytunnels. In

North America, the native common eastern bumblebee is similarly bred. Other native buzz pollinators include carpenter bees for cotton, and the southeastern blueberry bee (*Habropda laboriosa*).

In Australia, the *Trigona* group of stingless bees commercially pollinates macadamia nut, mango and watermelon. And in Central and South America, the potential for using stingless bees in the commercial production of many crops, including coffee, avocadoes, coconuts and tomatoes, is being investigated.

Throughout southern Asia, the eastern honeybee is the main managed pollinator, but wild giant honeybees partially pollinate cotton, mango, coconut and coffee, and farmers are also examining the role that their native stingless bees could play in modern agriculture. China is perhaps the largest provider of pollination ecosystems globally because it is home to most of the world's species of managed and wild honeybees, and boasts an incredible diversity of bumblebees and solitary bees. More than a fifth of the world's 250 bumblebee species have been recorded in the provinces of Gansu and Sichuan.

China has around 8 million hives (at least three or four times more than the United States); almost 3 million contain the native eastern honeybee and more than 5 million hives the western honeybee, first introduced as early as 1896. Yet, unlike the US and Europe, managed bee hives are not transported as much to pollinate orchards

Buzz pollination

Bumblebees, carpenter bees and flower bees can do something many other bees can't: buzz pollination. Tomatoes, aubergines (eggplants) and peppers are among the many fruits and vegetables that require this type of pollination.

When the bumblebee lands on such a plant, she wraps herself around the anthers and uses her flight muscles, without engaging her wings, to make her body vibrate. This movement, which shakes the pollen out of the anther's enclosure and onto the bee, makes an audible buzzing sound, hence the name.

and arable farms because farmers have traditionally relied on wild bees to pollinate crops.

The wild, dwarf and giant honeybee species are important pollinators, along with stingless bees, bumblebees and solitary bees which are uniquely diverse to China. Yet they are understudied with limited knowledge of their distribution across the vast country. The few studies that do exist point to alarming declines in wild bee populations in some areas of the country. In some cases, bees have been wiped out by the overuse of pesticides.

In a part of Sichuan, wild bees have not been seen since the mid-1980s and farmers are forced to pollinate their fruit crops by hand; a laborious and less efficient process than bee pollination.

Worldwide, bees have ensured humankind's survival by pollinating the food that we and our livestock eat. But now a number of man-made threats jeopardize their very existence – and with it, ours. This makes bees the modern-day canaries in the coalmine, warning us of imminent danger.

CHAPTER 3
Threats Facing Bees

✦ Bees on the edge ✦

Wild bees face a variety of external threats, often simultaneously. Their habitats have been destroyed over the last seventy years by intensive farming, urban sprawl and the widespread use of poisonous pesticides. At the same time, they are competing against invasive species that bring parasites and disease, and are vulnerable to the impact of climate change.

Across Europe, 24 per cent of the sixty-eight bumblebee species – nearly one in four – are threatened with extinction, and almost half have witnessed a decline in their populations. One of the most critically endangered is Cullum's bumblebee (*Bombus cullumanus*), named after Sir Thomas Cullum, a natural historian from Suffolk, UK where the bee was first described as a new species in 1802. It was found throughout western and central Europe, but in the last ten years, following habitat fragmentation and changes in farming practices which remove clovers, its main food, there has been an 80 per cent decline in this red-tailed bumblebee. The continent's largest bumblebee, the endangered *Bombus fragrans*, is also seriously threatened by the intensification of agriculture, which is destroying its native habitat on the steppes of Ukraine and Russia.

In the UK, six of the twenty-four different bumblebee species have recently declined by at least 80 per cent, including the shrill carder bumblebee (*Bombus sylvarum*), brown-banded carder bee (*Bombus humilis*), and the large garden bumblebee (*Bombus ruderatus*). All have long tongues to forage on deep-nectar flowers, which have disappeared as land is cleared to make way for large-scale farms or housing estates and shopping centres. One bumblebee now so rarely seen in the UK that it is considered vulnerable to extinction, is the great yellow bumblebee which is restricted to the clover-rich machair (sandy grasslands) unique to northern Scotland, the Hebrides and Orkney. The short-haired bumblebee (*Bombus subterraneus*) became extinct in the UK in 1989, until its reintroduction twenty-four years later (see page 181).

In North America, more than a quarter of its forty-six native bumblebees are at risk of extinction, including the iconically named American bumblebee (*Bombus pensylvanicus*), Franklin's bumblebee (*Bombus franklini*)

Franklin's bumblebee

and the rusty-patched bumblebee (*Bombus affinis*) which became officially recognized as endangered in 2017.

When it comes to solitary bees, there isn't enough data to know how at risk they may be. In Europe, for example, there's sufficient information on less than half the 2,000 or so species. Of these, 37 per cent have experienced a decline in populations and 9 per cent face extinction. Those most at risk are foragers who eat pollen from just one family of flowering plants, such as *Colletes anchusae* and *Colletes wolfi*, which only feed from the small, blue flowers of Barrelier's bugloss that grows wild in parts of eastern Europe, Turkey and Italy.

In 2017, the first ever review of all North America and Hawaii's 4,337 native bees found that of the 1,437 where an assessment was possible, almost a quarter were at increasing risk of extinction. Data deficiency makes it difficult to get a clear picture across Latin America, Africa, Asia and Oceania. Yet locally, worrying declines have been recorded.

The cumulative and interconnected perils that confront wild bees and other pollinators, and the unprecedented scale of the dangers they face, were identified in a groundbreaking report by the Intergovernmental Science-Policy Platform on Biodiversity and Ecosystem Services (IPBES) in 2016.

Managed European honeybees – on whom we increasingly rely for food production – are not immune to many of these threats. In the last decade, catastrophic annual losses of 40–50 per cent of colonies have been recorded in the US and Europe. Some of these losses have been attributed to colony collapse disorder, when bees disappear from their hives. Since US beekeepers first raised the alarm in 2006, a combination of poor nutrition, pesticides and parasites (all the direct result of industrial farming practices) have been identified as the likely culprits. Beekeepers have the option of restocking their hives by buying bees from commercial breeders, but wild bee species can't be so easily repopulated.

◆ Habitat loss ◆

It cannot be overestimated how far scientific and technological advances have revolutionized modern agriculture, successfully transforming farmers into large-scale industrialized food producers to feed billions of people. Yet that has come at an unacceptable cost to bees and other pollinators.

There is a dangerous contradiction at the heart of this system. It relies increasingly on insect pollinators – in the last five decades there has been a 300 per cent increase in the volume of production of ninety commercially grown crops that are dependent on these pollinators – but at the same time it is hastening their decline.

Hedgerows, which traditionally divided fields and provided nesting sites and forage, have been ripped up to make way for mega fields planted with one crop. Wild flowers, whose pollen and nectar can sustain bees throughout the summer, have been destroyed by weedkillers and artificial fertilizers that promote the growth of vigorous grasses. The switch from traditional haymaking at the end of the summer to producing silage earlier in the year to feed livestock has also been devastating for bees, such as the moss carder bee, as fields are mowed when clovers, alfalfa and other vetches are in full flower, robbing them of rich sources of food and nesting sites.

Bee abundance in the US has declined most sharply in the Midwest corn belt and Central Valley, California, where agriculture has greatly intensified. As wild bee populations decline, managed honeybees are expected to take up the slack. But a landscape full of one crop, be it almonds or sunflowers, doesn't provide the varied,

Moss carder bee

balanced diet that honeybees need to thrive. Sometimes the crops they are taken to pollinate are even harmful. Scientists have found that pollen from blueberries – a fruit that honeybees are forced to pollinate commercially – is too acidic for the larvae and could be a possible cause of bacterial brood infection.

Not surprisingly, honeybees are fitter and their populations grow faster where there is a continuous supply of nutritious forage. The same is true of stingless bees in the depleted forests of Central America. Where trees have been felled for livestock rearing or intensive agriculture, beekeepers report a lack of pollen and nectar sources from native forest trees as a probable cause for colony losses.

In the UK, where since the Second World War 97 per cent of grassland-rich wild flower meadows have either been replaced with monoculture farming or concreted over, there has been a dangerous decline in the number of bee species and their abundance due to a loss of floral diversity.

✦ Poisoned by pesticides ✦

The widespread use of chemicals to kill the numerous pests that can attack crops at various stages of their growth is a hallmark of modern arable farming. Yet many of these insecticides are also highly toxic to the beneficial insects that pollinate the crops.

Bees have been poisoned by pesticides ever since they were first invented. Rachel Carson, in her seminal book *Silent Spring* (1962), warned the world about their devastating impact on the environment. She described how cotton sprayed with arsenic killed most bees in the southern United States at the beginning of the twentieth century. Some fifty years later, synthetic pesticides – a by-product of chemical warfare – most notably DDT, were responsible for wiping out wildlife including birds and bees. Banned in the US in 1972, because of 'human cancer risks' and 'environmental hazards', similar pesticides continue to be widely used by farmers that are acutely toxic to bees, including Chlorpyrifos, a nerve agent first registered in 1965 by the company that manufactured Agent Orange (the toxic and deadly herbicide used by the US military to clear vegetation in the Vietnam War).

By the mid-1990s, a new class of pesticides called neonicotinoids were introduced. They are designed to be applied as a seed coating on a range of crops, from sunflowers to maize and oilseed rape, and systemically move through the plant from the seed to the shoots, stem, leaves and flowers, where they attack an insect's nervous system on contact or ingestion. They proved so lethal to crop predators that they swiftly became the most widely used insecticides in the world.

But, within a decade, neonicotinoids were coming under close scrutiny, associated with colony collapse disorder in the US and negative impacts on bees in Europe. Scientific studies have shown that honeybees in the field exposed to tiny doses of 'neonics', can experience reduced olfactory memory and learning performance and possibly impaired orientation skills, making it difficult for them to locate food sources and find their way home. Sublethal doses of the pesticides have also been shown to significantly reduce the growth rate of bumblebee colonies and the production of new bumblebee queens.

In 2013, the European Union adopted a partial ban on three widely used neonicotinoids – clothianidin, imidacloprid and thiamethoxam – because of their suspected danger to bees. The restrictions applied to crops including maize, wheat, barley, oats and oilseed rape.

Five years later, a large body of scientific evidence had linked 'neonics' with harmful effects on honeybees, bumblebees and the wider environment, and the EU made the ban permanent and extended it to all outdoor crops. However, their use is still permitted for agricultural purposes in greenhouses and in a range of domestic products and veterinary treatment for pets, such as flea collars.

Since the ban was declared, research has shown that bees can actually become addicted to these pesticides, returning frequently to the treated crops. Yet the pesticide manufacturers maintain that their products can't be held responsible for killing bees, and they are still widely applied to crops in most parts of the world.

It's not only toxic chemicals used by farmers that honeybees regularly come in contact with, beekeepers themselves have been treating their hives for many years with chemicals designed to control a parasitic mite, which left unchecked can spread lethal viruses.

• Invaders and parasites •

At the beginning of the twentieth century, Russian beekeepers began to transport their honeybees eastwards on the newly opened Trans-Siberian railway.

Unfortunately, a parasitic mite that had happily co-existed with the eastern honeybee in Asia over millions of years, jumped onto the Russians' bees with catastrophic consequences. The hapless western honeybee wasn't able to build up any defences against the varroa mite that debilitates the bees and vectors deadly viruses.

A little over a hundred years later, varroa has decimated western honeybees on every continent across the world except Australia, where the invaders have so far been kept out by strict import laws.

The mite looks like a tiny, reddish-brown dot on a small honeybee; but at about 1.1mm (0.04in) long and 1.5mm (0.06in) wide, living on a 14mm (0.6in) host, it is much bigger relative to the bee than a flea is to a dog. A better comparison would be a human being with a monkey on their back sucking their blood – and bees can often be host to more than one mite.

If left to their own devices, the bees would eventually come up with their own strategies to control the mite, but that could take thousands of years, and experiments on the Swedish island of Gotland suggest that varroaresistant colonies are smaller and fiercer, not ideal traits for managed pollinators.

As a beekeeper, one of the great joys is opening your hive after winter on the first warm spring day to find a strong, healthy colony. But the saddest sight is a dead colony, or one with only a few weak or diseased bees where varroa has clearly got the better of them. You feel you have failed in your custodial duties.

Varroa is a major cause of annual honeybee deaths worldwide. Every beekeeper has to weigh up the pros and cons of using chemicals or other methods, such as culling drones, to prevent varroa decimating the colony.

But these parasites are not the only example of the perils of moving bees around the world. Just as European settlers accidentally wiped out native populations in the Americas with a host of European diseases such as measles, bee immigrants, such as the European buff-tailed bumblebee, can transmit pathogens that kill native bees.

Buff-tailed bumblebee

In the early 1990s, two native North American bumble-bee species were sent to Europe to be reared commercially and were then imported back to pollinate in US greenhouses. Within fifteen years, four native bumblebee species had sharply declined, including the western bumblebee (*Bombus occidentalis*), which was one of the original commercial pollinators sent to Europe. The others are the yellow-banded bumblebee (*Bombus terricola*), the rusty-patched bumble-bee officially recognized as endangered, and Franklin's bumblebee, possibly the first US bumblebee to become extinct. Once abundant in the hills of southern Oregon and northern California, Franklin's bumblebee was last spotted on 9 August 2006. Robbin Thorp, the world's leading expert on this bumblebee, believes a disease carried by commercially bred buff-tailed bumblebees – which was picked up by their American cousins when they were being bred in Europe – escaped into the wild and is wiping out the natives.

In South America it's a similar story. Here, the giant golden bumblebee (see page 47), the only native bumblebee found in Patagonia, seems to have all but disappeared, less than twenty years after buff-tailed bumblebees arrived in Chile. This robust and highly adaptable European bumblebee escaped the greenhouses and has spread hundreds of miles across the Andes and into the southern half of Argentina. Along the way, it seems likely that it may have infected the giant bumblebees with a lethal disease.

Bee diseases and viruses can be transmitted between bees of different species on the flowers they visit. A healthy bee can come into contact with flowers that have been infected by a visiting bee. The petals can be contaminated by contact with her feet and body, and the nectar by her mouthparts. She can also leave parasites behind.

Exotic pests, such as the small hive beetle from Africa, are a threat to honeybees where they have turned up uninvited in shipping containers. African honeybees have evolved strong housecleaning and defensive traits that deny the beetle entrance to the hive, and any that do get in are locked in a prison made of propolis. In contrast, honeybees in North America and Australia are defenceless against the beetle and its offspring.

Similarly, in France, the Asian hornet has terrorized honeybees since it arrived in a package of Chinese pottery in 2004. It feeds its young on bee larvae and ransacks hives. In Asia, the eastern honeybee has evolved a unique defence to kill the hornets called heat balling. Several hundred bees surround the intruder in a tight ball and vibrate their muscles to produce a temperature of 46°C (115°F), which is hot enough to kill it. Western honeybees can't produce as high a heat and sting the intruder instead, which is much less effective.

The small, yellow-legged hornets have spread to northern Spain, the Channel Islands and the UK, where they were first spotted in Cornwall and Devon in 2016.

One of history's most spectacular examples of biological invasion has been greatly facilitated by rising climatic temperatures which encouraged the spread of the Africanized western honeybee (see page 68) from Brazil through Central America and into the southern states of America.

✦ Bees caught in a 'climate vice' ✦

Bees are threatened by the seemingly unrelenting increases in temperatures, a rise in the number and severity of extreme weather events, and the disruption in the timing of seasonal cycles – all manifestations of climate change.

Populations that cannot relocate are particularly vulnerable to extinction, such as the world's most northerly bumblebee, the Arctic bumblebee (see page 45) and Europe's second largest bumblebee, *Bombus hyperboreus*, whose habitats will become too warm. Projections show that other more widespread species, such as the apple bumblebee (*Bombus pomorum*), found across much of central and eastern Europe and Turkey, will only survive if it can move much further north to a small corner of Scandinavia.

Research that charted the locations of bee populations in North America and Europe between 1901 and 1974 found that many of the sixty-seven species analysed had been driven to the northernmost part of their geographical range because of rising temperatures leading to a contraction in their habitat by as much as 300km (186 miles).

Other research in the Rocky Mountains of Colorado showed over four decades that earlier spring snowmelt, warmer spring and summer temperatures, and more frequent damaging spring frosts had disrupted the finely tuned synchronicity between plant and pollinator, leading to a loss in abundance of three subalpine bumblebee species.

Extreme weather conditions such as hurricanes, floods and droughts also pose a threat. In Indonesia, the frequency of heavy rainfall has reduced food for the wild giant honeybee and decreased the population of these important pollinators of many locally grown crops. The increase in the number of hurricanes hitting Central America has wreaked devastation in areas where stingless bees are kept.

Drought is also bad news for bees. When less water is available to plants they invest less in reproduction, which means fewer flowers, less nectar and reduced sugar concentration in the nectar. In California, drought conditions are becoming a regular feature, forcing commercial beekeepers to move their bees up to Dakota and Montana to find forage. But many wild bees can't travel that far in search of food.

The Intergovernmental Science-Policy Platform on Biodiversity and Ecosystem Services (IPBES) warns that as climate change interacts with other pressures, such as habitat loss, overexploitation and invasive species, a large fraction of pollinator species may be at higher risk of extinction during the twenty-first century. It calls for urgent action to protect them.

✦ Loss of genetic diversity ✦

Bees have overcome many challenges during their 60 million years. Why are they finding these modern assailants so difficult to combat? One reason could be a loss of genetic diversity. At the beginning of the twentieth century, Brother Adam, a monk at Buckfast Abbey in Devon, cross-bred various different races of western honeybee to produce a bee with many desirable characteristics for beekeepers: gentle-natured, makes lots of honey and has low swarming tendencies. His Buckfast bee is still bred today all over the world, along with a handful of other docile races, including the Italian honeybee and Carniolan honeybee, originally from the Balkans. But honeybees with less attractive traits to humans may be better at adapting to the range of problems being thrown at them. In 2006, the western honeybee genome was fully sequenced, followed by the eastern honeybee in 2015. This allows today's commercial bee breeders to use genetic analyses to select for the perfect beekeepers' bee. But imperfect strains that have been passed over could contain within their DNA resistance to current and future foes.

✦ Disconnect with nature ✦

One of the biggest threats to bees is our lack of understanding about the natural world. Most of us have no idea how our food is produced and the vital role that pollinators' play. Humans tend to think they are outside of nature and that it is something to be enjoyed walking in the countryside at weekends or to be conquered with chemicals and large machinery.

Growing up in the 1970s, we remember our parents' car windscreen being splattered all over with insects during a drive into the countryside. Sometimes it was so bad, we would have to stop and clean it. At the time it seemed a terrible nuisance and we remember how our fathers' cursed. Now, that never happens. Why? A recent study in nature reserves across Germany, based on the work of dozens of amateur entomologists who began using standardized ways to collect flying insects in 1989, found that over a twenty-seven-year period more than three quarters had vanished. The annual average weight of the insects collected fell by 76 per cent, and the fall was even higher in summer – 82 per cent – when insect numbers reach their peak. Exposure to pesticides and lack of food are a likely explanation say scientists who were shocked by the scale of the losses. The huge decline has prompted warnings that the world is on course for 'ecological Armageddon', with profound impacts on humans.

Humankind, however, is part of nature. We may be at the top of the food chain, but if it starts to unravel because our actions are wiping out pollinators and the plants and animals that depend on them, we could soon follow. As John Muir, the Scottish founder of the conservation movement in the US, said: 'When one tugs at a single thing in nature, he finds it attached to the rest of the world.' By jeopardizing a lynchpin in the working of the planet, we are threatening the future of our world. But it's not too late to learn how to save the bees.

CHAPTER 4

Bees and How We Can Help Them

When it comes to saving endangered species, many of us wonder what role we can play. Making a difference can appear daunting and even impossible, especially for those of us living in towns and cities.

Yet, research has found some species of bumblebee seem to be more suited to urban areas where their colonies grow faster and are larger. A study in Nottingham, UK, comparing the diversity and abundance of solitary bees in urban and rural settings, found the green spaces (mainly churchyards, road verges, civic gardens and car parks) within a third of a mile of the city centre were home to more species and higher numbers of solitary bees than the nearby meadows and nature reserves. In total, forty-eight species were counted, 22 per cent of solitary bee species in the UK, including the nationally rare sharp-tailed bee *Coelioxys quadridentata*. Many keen naturalists are recording and monitoring bees in their local urban green spaces. An ecologist in north-east London, for example, has identified thirty-four solitary bee species in an overgrown cemetery, including the rarely seen four-banded flower bee (*Anthopora quadrimaculata*) and furry-clasped furrow bee (*Lasioglossum lativentre*). While in south-east London, a resident has photographed forty-four different species of bee in her local park, including a mining bee that is so

Five simple steps to help bees

- Plant year-round flowers, shrubs and trees for bees

- Provide nesting sites and materials

- Ditch the weedkillers and bug sprays

- Leave the mower in the shed

- Create a bee watering hole

rare it's called the scarce black mining bee (*Andrena nigrospina*).

Yet not all urban green spaces are bee-friendly. The trend of ripping up suburban front gardens to park cars, decking over backyards, or frequently mowing lawns is hugely detrimental to bees. But there are simple steps we can all take to help them. And one of the most rewarding aspects of helping bees is that small, simple actions can achieve large benefits. Some actions we can take alone, and others require joining with other like-minded people. So where do you start?

✦ Gardening for bees ✦

Gardens cover between a quarter and third of towns and cities, so *how* we garden could make a big difference. A garden full of lavender will be humming with bumblebees in June and July, but the same garden can be a bee desert months earlier when solitary bees that fly in cold weather are looking for pollen and larger bumblebee queens are in desperate need of nectar to fuel their search for a nest. The trick is to have a variety of flowers, shrubs and trees that together provide nectar and pollen throughout the year, especially as some bumblebees are now a common sight on mild winter days.

Hellebores, cyclamens and crocuses are examples of flowers that provide nectar and pollen at the beginning of the year, and heleniums and African daisies well into autumn. Cherry trees, pussy willow and mahonia bushes are also excellent early food sources.

One tip for buying bee-friendly plants is to visit a garden centre and just watch which flowers attract the bees. Many flowers are bred sterile, without pollen or nectar, such as colourful bedding plants and the ever-popular pelargoniums. (These are confusingly called geraniums, while true geraniums, known as hardy geraniums or cranesbill, are much loved by bees, and some varieties flower all summer.) Double-headed flowers, such as roses and pom-pom-style dahlias, may look spectacular, but they provide no easily accessible food. The general rule of thumb is to choose simple, daisy-like, or bowl-shaped flowers, which allow short-tongued bees easy pickings, bell-like flowers for bees with a longer proboscis, or flowers like sweet peas and vetches with a lip at the front that bees can use as a landing platform. And plant them in large clumps, as that's what the bees prefer.

Plants in many garden centres will come with a bee-friendly label attached. But check that any plants you buy haven't been treated with neonicotinoid pesticides that are linked to bee deaths worldwide (see page 148). There are many bee-friendly plant lists available but they don't tell you if the flowers are right for your garden, if they will flower in succession, or which species of bees will visit them. Some of that knowledge will only come from trial and error. Many of us are restricted in what we can successfully grow by soil type, the climate, the size of our outdoor space, how much sun it gets, and the creatures that already live there.

The key is to work with what you have. Rather than trying to grow sunflowers, lupins and open-faced dahlias if it entails waging a war against snails, plant bee-friendly flowers that gastropods won't devour, such as alliums, anise hyssop, and catmint. If you have heavy soil, add horticultural grit for better drainage to allow a variety of Mediterranean herbs to flourish in hot, dry summers, from rosemary in early spring, to chives, thyme and mint, right through to wild marjoram in late summer.

Bees prefer to forage in the sun, but if your garden is in shade for much of the day grow lungwort, bugle, cranesbill and Japanese anemone, and the bees will come.

Most flowers take time to replenish their nectar after being visited by a bee, but comfrey refills immediately making it a must for any bee garden from May through to September. Although it's an annual plant, it readily self-seeds and can grow with wild abandon. Gardeners will need to loosen up if they want to help bees. Some bee favourites, such as pretty sky-blue forget-me-nots, alkanet, and yellow dandelions, are loathed by gardeners who consider them troublesome weeds, turning up where they are not wanted. But a weed is just a plant in the wrong place, and they

Early-flowering pussy willow

often provide essential bee food before other flowers are in bloom. They can easily be pulled up, or dug up for those with a deep tap root, when they are no longer in flower.

A green lawn could feed bees if mown less frequently to allow the odd dandelion and clover to grow. Or it could be completely transformed into a bee-friendly lawn by sowing yellow rattle, a flower that is a parasite of grass and will create space for wild flowers and herbs to flourish, or prepared mixes of grasses and low-growing perennials such as white clover, creeping thyme and self-heal. And try covering the roof of a garden shed with a waterproof membrane, a thin layer of poor soil, and sprinkling wild flower seeds to create a meadow.

Trees are by far the most abundant source of pollen and nectar for urban honeybees. In early spring the workers collect pollen from catkins hanging from pussy willow trees, and nectar nestled in the blossom of cherry and plum trees, and in midsummer they make honey from the white flowers that cover mature lime trees dotting parks and streets in many towns and cities.

Even a small outdoor space can provide bees with tasty, nutritious meals year-round. Try turning a wall into a bee bar by putting up some trellis and growing climbing plants and creepers up it, such as honeysuckle, perennial sweet peas and bee-friendly clematis. Instead of a fence, erect a hedge made of bee-friendly shrubs that together will flower all year, such as winter-flowering *viburnum tinus*, followed by hazel, cotoneaster, and the strawberry tree bush. If you are looking to make your garden more intruder-proof, various thorny and prickly shrubs will deter burglars while feeding bees, such as holly whose tiny white flowers appear in early summer.

Hanging baskets, pots and window boxes if planted with suitable flowers and watered regularly can provide bee refreshments on patios, balconies, terraces and window ledges. Wild flowers sown in containers bloom in midsummer, so are best planted alongside spring bulbs and late summer perennials to ensure tasty bee snacks are available all year.

Research shows that bees visit native and non-native flowering plants. They don't care where they came from as long as they provide food.

If you want to help specific bees, generic plant lists or bee-friendly labels aren't much help. UK Horticulturalist Rosi Rollings set up a site for trialling plants at her Rosybee Nurseries in Oxfordshire, UK, to see which different bees seemed to like best. Averaged over five years, her top performers for bumblebees include viper's-bugloss, whose stunning spikes of blue flowers produce nectar all day (like other members of the borage family); a low-growing catmint, called *Nepeta racemosa*, with summer-long purple flowers that attract many bumblebee species; and Macedonian scabious *(Knautea macedonica)*, whose crimson, pincushion-like flowers provide forage into early autumn.

Geranium rozanne attracted the most solitary bees. Among those Rosi Rollings identified on its purple, saucer-like flowers are some of the tiny black bees that to the untrained eye can look like flies. They include the common furrow bee *(Lasioglossum calceatum)*, the chalk furrow bee *(Lasioglossum fulvicorn)*, and the 6mm (0.2in) large scissor bee *(Chelostoma florisomne)*. The yellow daisy-like flowers of *Anthemem tinctoira*, also known as dyer's chamomile, were the second most popular, attracting yellow-legged mining bees (*Andrena flavipes*); ashy mining bees (*Andrena cineraria*); bare-saddled plasterer bees (*Colletes similis*); and bronze furrow bees (*Halictus tumulorum*). Low catmint was a hit with mason bees and the painted mining bee (*Andrena fucata*), while campanulas (also known as bellflowers) hosted a number of tiny visitors from the small scissor bee, whose scientific name *Chelostoma campanularum* indicates her flower preference, to Smeathmean's furrow bee *(Lasioglossum smeathmanellum)*, which is almost hairless with a metallic green sheen, and the white-jawed yellow face bee (*Hylaeus confusus*).

Surprisingly, several of the longest flowering and popular bee plants in Rosi's study, such as Sneezeweed (*Helenium 'Sahins early flower')* and the white spikes of Lavender 'Edelweiss' are sterile. They produce nectar, but not pollen, and keep generating more and more flowers in a futile attempt to reproduce.

✦ Water ✦

As well as nectar, bees also need to drink water. Once you have turned your garden into a bee magnet, provide a watering hole for them. A shallow bowl full of water and stones or pebbles on which the bees can stand while they are drinking will suffice. If you have a pond, make sure there is plenty of floating vegetation. Bees can't swim, so without landing boards or standing stations it is a potential death trap.

✦ Nesting sites ✦

Wild bees, unlike honeybees, forage close to home, so they need suitable nesting sites nearby. Artificial bee hotels for cavity-nesting mason and leafcutter bees are easy to make.

DIY bee hotel

You will need

Garden twine, or wire; a plastic 1-litre drinks bottle or a 20cm (8in) length of plastic drain pipe with a diameter of 10–15cm (4–6in); bamboo canes around 5–15mm (up to 0.5in) diameter, or similar tubes made out of cardboard; a scalpel, a small saw, a hammer and nail.

How to make your bee hotel

Cut the neck off the water bottle, or trim the drainpipe, so it's about 20cm (8in) in length, make two small incisions on either side of the length of the bottle/pipe and thread through enough twine or wire to make a loop for hanging the hotel. Cut the bamboo canes into lengths a little shorter than the bottle/pipe. Ensure the cane is hollow and without a nodule in the middle. You can buy cut bamboo cane, or 15mm (0.5in) cardboard tubes lined with paper.

Tightly wedge the canes, or tubes, into the bottle/pipe. You may need to push some smaller twigs or plant stems in to wedge them firmly in.

Where to put it

Ideally a south-facing wall sheltered from the wind and in full sun, not shaded by overhanging vegetation. Suspend the bee hotel at least 1m (1 yard) off the ground, with a slight tilt so that rain does not enter the canes or tubes. Drill the nail into the wall and securely attach with the twine or wire.

When to put it up

In spring, before the apple tree blossoms.

How do you know if it is being used?

You may see bees coming and going with pollen on their abdomens, or carrying pieces of mud, or leaf. When a mason bee has laid six or seven eggs in a cane, or tube, she will seal it with mud, and a leafcutter will do the same with masticated leaf later in the summer.

Other material the bees need

A patch of bare, damp earth for red mason bees. They will collect the mud and use it to partition the tubes into individual birth chambers, and to seal each tube. Leaves for the leafcutter bees to partition and seal their nest.

We have attached eight bee hotels under the eaves of our garden shed. The hotels face south and overlook our neighbour's overgrown garden covered in green alkanet and dandelions when mason bees emerge in late spring. Another neighbour grows roses. Last year for the first time we also attached a wooden solitary bee observation nest box with two removable shutters, which allows a fascinating window into the bees' world. You can see adults constructing birthing chambers, and the brood in different stages of development: eggs, larvae grubs eating pollen and spinning a cocoon. A dozen different solitary bee species have been recorded using nest boxes.

Other nesting sites can be created for a variety of solitary bees by: drilling long holes into blocks of wood, for wool carder or resin bees; piling up old turf or soil to make a south-facing bank of loose soil for mining bees; or by leaving crumbling walls for flower bees, mining bees or furrow bees to nest in the old mortar.

If you have a large enough outside space, you could make a four-storey bee hotel from wooden pallets placed on top of each other and crammed with wooden logs drilled with holes, cut bundles of bamboo, hay or straw, and topped with tiles or turf to keep out the rain.

Don't forget to have other nesting material at hand, for example tiny pieces of gravel or substrate for resin bees, and clumps of lamb's ear for wool carder bees.

✦ Bumblebee nests ✦

Bumblebees also require nesting sites. Unfortunately, they often spurn man-made bumblebee boxes. Our attempts to create a suitable cavity by placing an upturned flowerpot or teapot on the soil have failed. We have read that they will enter through the spout of the teapot, or through a piece of hose placed under a flowerpot, left protruding from the earth. Since many bumblebees like to nest in vacant rodent holes, maybe we would have had more success if we had packed the space with recycled bedding material from a mouse cage; it makes sense that the smell of mice could attract them.

For those that prefer to nest just above ground in a pile of old leaves or long grass, leave an area of garden untidy and undisturbed. Bumblebees can also sometimes be found nesting in compost bins, so why not create a small compost heap especially for them? They should vacate by the end of the summer when the colony dies, and then the compost can be used for garden mulch. For those high-rise nesters that colonize bird boxes after the chicks have fledged, try putting up more boxes for bees. When the birds return, the colony should have died out.

✦ City refuge for bees ✦

One of the reasons bees are thought to be faring better in cities than the countryside is that pesticide use is lower in urban areas. Paris, for example, banned pesticides for municipal and personal use more than a decade ago. Seattle, Copenhagen and Tokyo have also ditched them. Yet the world's most widely used chemical, glyphosate (brand name, RoundUp), is still sprayed by many councils to stop weeds growing through cracks in the pavements and by gardeners who want a weed-free lawn. This is despite research suggesting it could be contributing to the global bee decline.

If everyone living in a city of, say, 1 million people turned their gardens, backyards or roof terraces into havens for wild bees, they could form rivers of flowers flowing through the urban landscape that would act as important bee feeding stations. But gardening is not enough. We need to encourage our employers to install planters and bee hotels on their office roofs, and our childrens' schools to make their grounds more bee-friendly – there are many examples all over the world of pupils growing fruits and vegetables and learning about pollinators. Moreover, we must explain to our local councillors why managing municipal green spaces with pollinators, as well as people, in mind is a vote-winner. Councillors often report that residents demand neat, tidy, regularly mowed lawns but if given the option of well-managed, colourful wild flower meadows, or beds of attractive bee-friendly perennials alongside information about why this style of gardening better helps bees (most of whom won't sting), residents are generally enthusiastic. Gardening for bees can also be a cheaper option. We can encourage councils to plant more trees for bees in streets and parks. Decisions about which trees to plant rarely consider their value to pollinators. But we can change that decision process.

Urban landscaping to support pollinators is slowly becoming more mainstream, led by top garden designers such as Piet Oudolf, who brought his trademark native prairie style to Lurie Garden in Chicago and the High Line in Manhattan, and Nigel Dunnett who created the stunning wild flower meadows at London's Olympic Park.

Urban redevelopment efforts have historically prioritized economic opportunities and outcomes. Cities have been viewed as outside nature. Now, however, as more wildlife – not just bees – is migrating to them in search of food and shelter, findings from urban ecology suggest that planners should reconsider the urban core's possibilities for biodiversity conservation and ensure this is reflected in new developments. In some cities, including San Francisco and Toronto, it is now law that any new building has to include a green roof to help mitigate against flooding, improve air quality and cool down the city. If planted with year-round forage, and hosting nesting sites, they could also provide important bee habitat. Ecologists and wildlife organizations are devising ways to join up newly created but fragmented patches to create an infrastructure of bee corridors, or B-lines.

Cities are also crucial to the future of bees because they are where most people now live. Here urban citizens can learn about the importance of bees; interact with them; learn how to identify them by volunteering for conservation charities; participate in monitoring projects and habitat-creation schemes together with neighbours or local community groups; and join initiatives such as the Million Pollinator Garden Challenge in the US, or Urban Buzz in the UK. Cities are where advocacy for pollinators has to be built. Only when people have come to value, appreciate and be amazed by the many different bee species will they care enough to try to save them.

Honeybees became a cause célèbre for environmental charities and campaigning organizations in the first decade of the twenty-first century, when colony collapse disorder hit the headlines. Millions signed petitions lobbying politicians for action to save apian pollinators, which governments couldn't ignore.

National pollinator strategies were issued in some countries setting out steps for protecting pollinators in towns, cities and the countryside. In 2018, an EU-wide pollinator initiative was launched that includes action plans to help its members protect the habitats of the most threatened pollinating insects.

✦ Farming for bees ✦

These measures alone won't save bees. Food production has to change. Subsidies from governments and international agencies have over the past seventy years encouraged large-scale industrial agriculture to produce cheap food to feed billions of people, at the expense of wild bees and other pollinators.

There are glimmers of hope. Over the last thirty years, in the UK, more than 30,000km (18,641 miles) of hedgerows have been restored by farmers and wild flower habitat the equivalent of 10,000 football pitches has been created. In many countries, some farmers are working with conservation charities to increase pollinator habitat for wild bees, mainly as an insurance policy against shortages of honeybees. Since 2006, when honeybee numbers crashed in the US, 27,000 acres of almond orchards have been planted with wild flowers in Central Valley, California. But it's still less than 3 per cent of the 1 million acres of almond trees. Research shows that if one farm creates bee habitat but is surrounded by a sea of farmland growing crops in a conventional way, its efforts to attract enough wild bees to pollinate its crops will fail.

So how can we influence how our food is grown or our countryside managed to protect bees? The successful campaigns orchestrated against the use of certain pesticides in Europe clearly show that when millions of people lobby politicians it can bring about massive change. These campaigns focused on honeybees, but now we need more action to save wild bees. What if weedkillers were banned and farmers had to grow wild flowers alongside pesticide-free crops and provide nesting sites for bees? We also have clout as consumers. What if we refused to eat blueberries or almonds unless they carried a bee-friendly label?

What if we sat down with food producers, manufacturers and retailers and explained our concerns, then together tried to come up with solutions, such as putting in place throughout the food supply chain action to protect bees and other pollinators? We may have to be prepared to pay a little more for our food if we don't want bees harmed in the making of it.

In Minnesota – the fifth leading farming state in the US – a citizen stakeholder task force including representatives from farmers' groups, the pesticide industry, landscapers, beekeepers and pollinator campaigners was set up in 2016 by the then governor to help advise him on measures to support pollinators. Not surprisingly, the members didn't always see eye to eye, but nevertheless they recommended that farmers urgently receive state financial aid and technical support to make their practices more pollinator-friendly, such as being paid to stop using seed treated with neonicotinoid pesticides.

There is plenty of guidance for farmers who want to take voluntary action to support pollinators. Research shows that the greater the diversity of bees attracted to a field of crops by the presence of wild flowers, the better pollinated those crops will be. In some trials harvests doubled or even tripled for crops including pumpkins, courgettes (zucchini) and tomatoes. But there hasn't been enough government cash to make pollinator-friendly farming viable for most farmers.

We can lobby for change. In Bavaria, a petition to radically change the south German state's farming practices was signed by more than 1 million people in early 2019. Politicians will not be able to ignore its demands for 20 per cent of farming land to be made bee-friendly within six years and 30 per cent by 2030, in order to reverse the serious decline in flora and fauna.

✦ Rewilding ✦

In a successful example of rewilding, Knepp estate, a 3,500 acre farm in West Sussex, UK, used to receive substantial subsidies to produce milk and crops using conventional farming practices that degraded the land and destroyed ecosystems. Now it receives £250,000 a year of UK taxpayers' money to allow nature to restore ecosystems and the habitats within it. A decade after fences were removed on the farm and large grazing animals were introduced, sixty-two species of bee, including seven of national importance, have been recorded in the open fields, where wild flowers, vetches, clovers, fleabane and ragwort all now flourish, and dense thickets of sallow, hawthorn and blackthorn have taken root. Some of the rarer species, such as the red bartsia bee (*Melitta tricincta*) and *Melitta europaea*, which only visits yellow loosestrife, are specialists in particular flowers that now grow wild at Knepp.

Its owners believe other farmers could be incentivized to create rewilding on small parcels of land for twenty-five-year periods on a rotational system to bring back wildlife-rich scrub and boost populations of pollinators.

If enough habitats were returned to this state could some of the wild bees that have become extinct be reintroduced?

✦ Reintroducing extinct bees ✦

In Britain, short-haired bumblebees have been successfully reintroduced twenty-four years after they were last seen. The reason for this success is twofold: habitat creation and a healthy population of the reintroduced species. Farmers and landowners worked for many years with conservation charities to turn 1,300 hectares of marshes and farmland into flower-rich habitat, receiving grants to put whole fields into red clover leys, others to sow strips of wild flowers along field margins, or to undertake major meadow restoration projects. The original plan was to bring back the descendants of the British short-haired bumblebees taken to New Zealand in 1885, but they were found to be inbred, with a dangerously low level of genetic diversity, and unlikely to survive. Luckily, stronger short-haired bumblebees were found in Sweden and reintroduced instead. Just as excitingly, other rare bumblebees have returned to the area: the shrill carder bee after a twenty-five-year absence; the ruderal bumblebee (*Bombus ruderatus*)

Short-haired bumblebee on clover

after a decade; the red-shanked carder bee has also made a comeback; and the brown-banded carder bee and moss carder bee (*Bombus muscorum*), which was thought to be practically extinct, have seen a resurgence.

Unfortunately, in most cases reintroducing species is not a panacea for saving bees from extinction because many species of wild bee, such as Franklin's bumblebee and the rusty-patched bumblebee of North America, are localized and not found anywhere else (see page 142). Lack of food is not always the cause of their demise; sometimes diseases spread by introduced bees, or a change in the climate, is the problem so no amount of wild-flower sowing will bring them back.

٭ The way forward ٭

On our exciting journey of discovery from urban bee-keepers to cheerleaders for wild bees, we have come to better appreciate the wondrous workings of nature. It is an intricate, rich tapestry: complex, interconnected, amazing, surprising and at times baffling. But one thing has become abundantly clear to us: the good bee plays a key role in this life support system. Their pollination of flowering plants gives us the oxygen that we breathe and the food that we eat, as well as providing sustenance and shelter for the birds and mammals with whom we share this planet.

The bee carries a lot of weight on its tiny shoulders. But this crucial co-dependency that keeps us all alive is fragile, and facing grave and imminent peril. We urgently need to take a fresh look at the small things around us in an effort to understand the bigger picture. As the nineteenth century poet, William Blake, put it: 'To see a world in a grain of sand, and a heaven in a wild flower.'

Only when we really get to know and love some of the many bee species, in all their many guises, can we begin to help them. And then, perhaps, we can save these amazing creatures on whose existence our own depends, before it is too late.

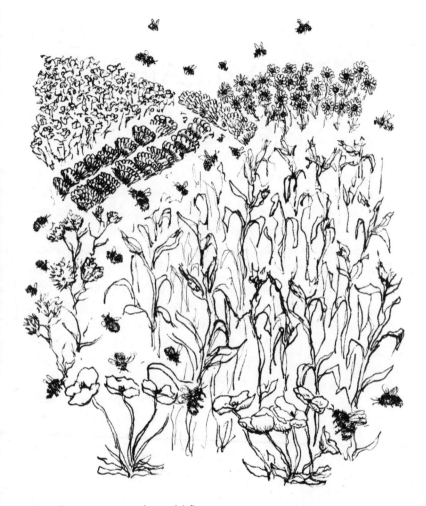

Bees enjoying the wild flowers growing among crops

About the Authors

Alison Benjamin and Brian McCallum are authors of the bestselling *A World Without Bees* (2008), *Keeping Bees and Making Honey* (2008), and *Bees in the City* (2011). Alison is an editor at the *Guardian* and Brian is a commercial beekeeper and former government bee inspector. Together they co-founded Urban Bees, which maintains a number of corporate rooftop bee hives, solitary bee hotels and bee-friendly gardens, educates people about bees and nature and promotes better forage and habitat. Its Regent's Park apiary also produces the finest honey. Urban Bees is a member of the Honey Club, which developed the award-winning King's Cross Bee Trail App, and it partnered with River of Flowers to create a solitary bee garden at the RHS Chelsea Flower Show 2018. Alison and Brian are married, live in Hackney, East London, and find bees endlessly fascinating.

More information at **www.urbanbees.co.uk**

Acknowledgements

Thanks to: Kathryn Lwin for her inspiration. Penny Metal for introducing us to many small solitary bees, photographed for her amazing book, *Insectinside, life in the bushes of a small Peckham park*. Rosi Rollings for generously sharing her research into the attractiveness of flowers to specific bee species at www.rosybee.com. Paul Feldman for his diligent research for this book. Andy Bodle for his invaluable editing skills. Gabriella Nemeth at Michael O'Mara Books, and the publisher for giving us the opportunity to write *The Good Bee*. And friends and family for their encouragement and support.

Select Bibliography

Benton, T., *Solitary Bees Naturalists' Handbooks 33*, Pelagic Publishing, 2017

Embry, P., *Our Native Bees: North America's endangered pollinators and the fight to save them*, Timber Press, 2018

Falk, S., *Field Guide to the Bees of Great Britain and Ireland*, Bloomsbury, 2015

Goulson, D., *Bee Quest*, Jonathan Cape, 2013

Metal, P., *Insectinside, life in the bushes of a small Peckham park*, 2017, https://insectinside.me

Michener, C., *Bees of the World*, John Hopkins University Press, 2000

Tautz, J., *The Buzz about Bees: Biology of a Superorganism*, Springer, 2008

Tree, I., *Wilding: The Return of Nature to a British Farm*, Picador, 2018

Von Frisch, K., *The Dancing Bees: An Account of the Life and Senses of the Honey Bee*, Methuen, 1954

Index

Page numbers in *italic* refer to illustrations